EVALUATION RESEARCH AS A FEEDBACK MECHANISM FOR CRIMINAL JUSTICE POLICY MAKING: A CRITICAL ANALYSIS

RICHARD P. SEITER

San Francisco, California
1978

Published By

R & E Research Associates, Inc.
4843 Mission Street
San Francisco, California 94112

Publishers

Adam S. Eterovich
Robert D. Reed

Library of Congress Card Catalog Number

77-94147

ISBN

0-88247-528-2

TABLE OF CONTENTS

CHAPTER I

INTRODUCTION

General Problem to be Addressed

The American correctional scene is in an unstable and transitional state. Not since the 1790's, when the correctional institution developed as a refuge in which to place criminal offenders, has the field of corrections undergone such pronounced policy changes. In the 1970's another radical change in correctional policy originated; this change is characterized by a movement back to keeping the offender in the community rather than isolating him in a prison.

The growing realization of the egregious and dysfunctional effects of institutionalization in the rehabilitation of offenders has produced an excrescence of community correctional programs. This present emphasis on community corrections is based on the proposition that in order to relieve society of the crime problem (in the long run), the problem must be attacked at its origin -- the community. Therefore, efforts are being made to reintegrate ex-offenders into the culture in which they will be living following their release from correctional supervision.

Rehabilitation has been proven limited in effectiveness when attempted in a deleterious institutional atmosphere that attempts to proscribe individualism and initiative, while sustaining dependency and inefficiency. The concensus in corrections is that the offender can be guided along the path of productive citizenship by emphasizing and building community ties, becoming involved in vocational and other community programs, and yet maintaining the supervisory and deterrent role of corrections.[1]

Changes in correctional philosophy and policy have led to the development of new community programs and the expansion of present ones. However, the surge of community programs has not been the result of a rational or synoptic policy analysis, but has resulted from pressure to change the prior policy due to its ineffectiveness.

Therefore, it may be suggested that a rational policy analysis be applied to the present surge of community corrections. Some have perhaps advocated community corrections as a panacea for offender reintegration without carefully analyzing the clients, his needs and capabilities, and available services and programs to fulfill these needs. Although the basic philosophy of community corrections appears to have efficacious possibilities, radical policy changes should not be developed haphazardly. Community correctional administrators should not be subject to the pitfalls that, due to a lack of analysis and evaluation, have perplexed correctional programs for years.

The importance of evaluation and systematic policy analysis (especially in developing programs such as community corrections) cannot be underestimated. The President's Commission on Law Enforcement and Administration of Justice indicated an acute awareness of this need:

> The most conspicuous problems in corrections today are lack of knowledge and unsystematic approach to the development of programs and techniques . . . .
> . . .Failure to attempt really systematic research and evaluation of various operational programs has led to repetitive error. Even more, it has made it impossible to pinpoint the reasons for success when success did occur.[2]

A salient example of the present problem of non-rational policy analysis in community corrections is reflected in a statement taken from an LEAA technical assistance publication regarding halfway houses -- one type of community correctional program now receiving increasing attention:

> However, halfway houses must also commence qualitative research on the effectiveness of their programs. This is necessary both because those in the field of corrections and governmental funding agencies are increasingly inquiring into the quality of such programs, and also because halfway house administrators cannot afford to base programmatic judgements on "cumulative experience" or "intuition". Virtually the whole field of criminal justice has always been in this position. Halfway houses must avoid this vicious circle of perpetuating something which may well be ineffective or not changing

a program which is not as effective as it could be.[3]

The above statement could be applied to all areas of community corrections. We are presently at a transitional point in moving from institutional corrections to community corrections. Whereas once the prison and reformatory were the most often used correctional mode, if present trends continue, community programs will become the major modality for channeling offenders, while the institution will be used only as an alternative of "last resort".

This transitional period needs to be approached in both a systematic and empirical manner. "Accountability" should be the key word in the next few years of correctional planning. Rather than starting and continuing programs only for the sake of continuation, the field of corrections should recognize program failures, learn from their ineffectiveness, and develop alternatives.

With an emphasis on "experimental projects", one could argue that correctional administrators should implement innovative programs, work to keep them operating efficiently, and then objectively evaluate them to determine whether they merit continuance. If such programs do not prove to be effective, they should be discontinued and other experimental programs tried.

A method of determining program effectiveness and development of new programs is "systematic experimentation". Rivlin suggests that through systematic experimentation of innovative programs, programs are initiated in several sreas to establish a capacity to determine the conditions under which they work best, evaluated objectively, and the information about their effectiveness or non-effectiveness disseminated for use by other areas and jurisdictions.[4]

Although determination of policy from program evaluation seems logical, criminal justice programs are often started and continued even when the program is not accomplishing its stated objectives. However, this seemingly inefficient management is not solely the responsibility of the program administrator; the pressures under which he operates must also be examined. Within the "fishbowl" operations of public programs, it is more difficult to accept failure and make changes than in the private sector.

The criminal justice system is especially sensitive to failures. The prospect of a convicted rapist being treated in the community, rather than behind bars, is certainly not one with which the public is in agreement. The sensationalism of the offender returned to the community only to commit again the same crime is frequently exploited to its fullest by the mass media. However, the successful return of an offender will seldom merit even a few brief words in the modes of media.

Elected officials who rely on public support also pressure administrators to present successful programs. There are few times that a correctional agency will admit that a tax-supported program has failed in its endeavor to reduce crime. A combination of pressure from the public and elected officials often forces even the most competent and dedicated correctional administrator to compromise his objectivity in evaluating programs to which he has devoted a large amount of time and effort.

Such hurdles facing experimental programs need to be addressed and overcome. The public, elected officials, and administrators need to realize that community corrections has not reached a state of the art where there is a "sure fire" program to rehabilitate offenders. Community corrections may never reach its highest potential without experimental programs, objective research, and accountability to program efficacy.

The above points suggest the definite need for more rational policy-making during the transition toward community-based corrections. Research and program evaluation should be conducted to determine the consequences of possible alternatives. Programs already implemented must be tested for accountability; if they show that they are ineffective, serious consideration should be given to other alternative programs and their possible consequences.

Evaluative techniques that provide the analyst with information upon which to recommend policy are needed in the correctional field. Traditionally, program evaluation has not been extensively utilized in the policy-making process, due not only to the lack of interest in evaluation by the administrator, but also to the utilization of inappropriate evaluative techniques by the evaluator.

The following analysis is an attempt to develop evaluative techniques which permit results useful for decision making, and to illustrate possible policy alternatives which can result from such evaluation. The emphasis is on using program evaluation as a planning instrument. For planning purposes, an evaluation must lend itself to providing data that are conducive to planning, rather than to simple formulation of statements regarding the effectiveness of a program.

Significance of the Problem

There could be several untold results if policy makers were to continue to develop programs without emphasizing research, evaluation, and accountability. The least preferable consequence is that community correctional programs would become as ineffective as the prior policy of institutionalizing offenders.

It is an important historical lesson to note that institutions developed for basically the same reasons that community corrections are now becoming the major treatment modality for offenders -- the ineffectiveness and inhumanity of the previous system. Rothman, in his classic description of the movement to institutions in America, stated, "A repulsion from the gallows rather than any faith in the penitentiary spurred the late eighteenth-century construction".[5]

From 1790 to 1970 the institution was the most widely used treatment modality for offenders. Although the underlying purpose for developing a system of institutions to replace corporal punishment as a treatment of criminals was a human one, the reform was found to be ineffective in rehabilitating these offenders. A lack of analysis and evaluation have lead to a continuation of institutional programs that could not be defended in terms of outcome. This is a good example of how programs could regress rather than progress in their ability to assist clients, due to absence of feedback through evaluative analysis.

The importance of this discussion of the development of

institutional corrections lies in its relevancy to the development
of community corrections. While community corrections developed
as a response to the ineffectiveness and inhumanity of the prior
policy, there is again a lack of analysis of alternatives or
evaluations of community programs. Such analysis would be beneficial to the development of effective programs.

Although the author is in agreement with the underlying theory
and alleged economic benefits of community correctional programs,
there is doubt that these programs can reach the potential possible when policies are subjected to a rational decision-making
process. Without evaluation and accountability, it is possible
that historians will look back upon the era of the 1970's as a
period of yet another ineffective attempt at reform in corrections,
which later resulted in a return to the previous over-use of
institutions.

Another problem in the utilization of evaluations for development of policy is the inappropriate instrumentation used in
evaluation of correctional programs. The traditional measures of
outcome do not provide results which contribute to policy making,
therefore the optimal use of evaluation as a tool for policy analysis has not been reached. It could be argued that if evaluations
do not become more pragmatic in their concern for administrative
decision making, the credibility of evaluations will further de-
cline. Practitioners may further spurn the use of evaluations as
relevant and useful instruments in determining policy.

History Impinging on the Problem

It is sometimes felt that corrections in the community is a
by-product of the "new penology" which has arisen during the past
three decades. While advances in correctional research, particularly in the last twenty years, have illustrated the deleterious
effects of institutionalization, the establishment of the Law
Enforcement Assistance Administration (LEAA) in 1968 has supplied
a funding base to encourage innovative programs and broaden the
role of community corrections. However, the concept of treating

offender in a community setting is certainly not a new idea.

Documentation can be found that the need for treatment in the community was perceived as early as 1817. In that year, the Massachusetts Prison Commission recommended a temporary refuge to house destitute released offenders. The Commission had reached this conclusion after extensively surveying the State prison system and discovering that a substantial majority of the individuals then incarcerated in the institutions were recidivists. Included in their numerous recommendations for prison reform presented to the Massachusetts legislature was a suggestion that the State develop what would now be referred to as a "halfway house". The Commission proposed:

> . . . a building to be erected of wood, at a small expense as it is only recommended by way of experiment. The convicts who are discharged are often entirely destitute. The natural prejudice against them is strong, that they find great difficulty in obtaining employment. They are forced to seek shelter in the lowest receptacles; and if they wish to lead a new course of life, are easily persuaded out of it and perhaps driven by necessity to the commission of fresh crimes. It is intended to afford a temporary shelter in this building, if they chose to accept it, to such discharged convicts as may have conducted themselves well in prison at a cheap rate, and have a chance to occupy themselves in their trade, until some opportunity offers a placing of themselves where they can gain an honest livelihood in society. A refuge of this kind, to this destitute class, would be found perhaps humane and politic.[6]

Although the first halfway house in the United States did not become operational until 1864, the idea and practices for easing the transition between the institution and the community had gained a firm foothold in correctional progress.

Probation is believed to have developed in 1841, when John Augustus, a Boston Shoemaker, asked the magistrate to put offenders under his supervision, rather than putting them in jail. In 1878, Massachusetts passed a probation statute, and shortly thereafter, Rhode Island became the first state to have state-administered probation with supervision. It was not, however, until 1956 that all states had passed probation statutes for adults.[7]

Parole was first implemented in the United States in 1876, when the Elmira Reformatory in New York adopted the "Irish system" of corrections. This included both an indeterminant sentence, with time off for good behavior, and release on parole with supervision. Now more than 60 percent of adult felons in the United States are released on parole prior to the expiration of the maximum term of their sentences.[8] This brief historical sketch shows corrections in the community as not a new concept, although one which is now receiving a more appropriate share of correctional resources.

As stated above, there has been little program evaluation or research to document that community-based corrections is more effective than institutional corrections. A recent article which reviewed evaluations of halfway houses could discover no conclusive evidence of the effectiveness of such programs. In fact, the authors conclude:

> In terms of recidivism, the measuring rod traditionally used for determining the effectiveness of correctional programs, halfway house programs do not appear to have produced significantly better results than many community supervision programs, and in fact, in some instances have demonstrated a rather inferior performance.[9]

Although the underlying theory of community corrections appears to be sound, without development of more realistic outcome measures and relevant evaluation of programs, community corrections may be subjected to the same lack of comprehensive planning that has caused the ineffectiveness of institutional corrections.

Specific Project to be Addressed

In order to illustrate the use of program evaluation for gathering information as an instrument for rational decision-making, a study of the program, policies, and effectiveness of Ohio adult halfway houses has been conducted. Initially, demographic, offense, and other data were gathered indicating the types of offenders presently being placed in halfway houses and the services provided to them. Several steps have been taken to examine the policy and operations of halfway houses. After analysis of house goals, the evaluation focuses on the effectiveness of the present policy in reintegrating offenders, a cost comparison between present and alternative policies, and an analysis of the probable effects of possible policy changes on halfway house loads.

The basic target group for the study will include the eight halfway house systems[10] presently approved, certified, and partially funded by the Ohio Department of Rehabilitation and Correction, and the adult offenders who utilize these halfway house services. Private and other federal programs also financially support these facilities, which are part of the non-governmental (private) area of the criminal justice system. The included halfway houses and their locations are listed below:

Ralph W. Alvis House	Columbus
The Bridge Home for Young Men	Elyria
Denton House	Akron
Fellowship House	Toledo
Fresh Start, Inc.	Cleveland
Helping Hand Halfway Home, Inc.	Cleveland
Talbert House	Cincinnati
Vander Meulen House	Mansfield

Originally, halfway houses were established only as transitional programs to facilitate the re-entry into society of previously incarcerated offenders. However, the target population for halfway house services has greatly expanded in the last decade. A recent LEAA technical assistance publication lists eight current uses of community based treatment facilities:[11]

1. <u>As a transitional refuge for the mandatory releasee and parolee</u>

This is the traditional rationale of servicing a previously incarcerated group to ease their transition back into free society and to buffer the many negative effects of their period of incarceration and isolation from the community.

Previously, this group of clients was received directly upon release from the institution. Community centers are now being used for these persons who are having difficulty adjusting "on the street", and stand the risk of revocation of parole or return to the institution. The community center offers an alternative with intensive treatment and supervision in an attempt to break the "Prison-parole-prison" cycle.

2. As an alternative to incarceration for the probationer

Probationers are referred to a halfway house under two sets of general circumstances. First, the court may consider the individual too great of a risk to place them on a probation caseload where they will not receive the required intensive supervision or treatment. However, this individual could benefit from community placement and does not need institutional incarceration. The individual may then be placed in a residential facility as a condition of probation.

Second, an individual may already be on probation and experiencing adjustment problems. Again, the halfway house may provide the needed intensive treatment and supervision.

3. For the pre-release before his actual parole or mandatory release

Under current federal law, a federal prisoner may be released from thirty to one hundred and twenty days before his actual release date. He may then be placed in a community facility until his release date in order to utilize community resources to find a job, re-establish family ties, or find suitable housing.

4. To provide study and diagnostic services to offenders

Some of the more sophisticated halfway houses are able to provide courts with study and diagnostic services prior to final disposition. The offender may be placed in a halfway house for "study and observation" to discover problems and suggest recommendations for treatment and final disposition.

5. As group homes for the neglected: and delinquent juvenile

Group homes for the delinquent child serve several purposes. First, they give the court of jurisdiction an alternative to incarceration if the child does not respond to the supervision of his probation officer or social worker. Second, the group home may be used as a short-term facility for the delinquent child, while community services and counseling attempt to remedy his problems. Third, the group home is also used as a "halfway out" facility for children who have been incarcerated and do not have an adequate home plan.

6. <u>For individuals with special difficulties such as drug abuse, alcoholism, and psychiatric problems</u>

Due to the nature of the problems, the stay at centers servicing individuals with drug abuse, alcoholism, and psychiatric problems is often much longer than at those units servicing the general offender population. Many of these centers utilize some variant of the therapeutic community technique.

7. <u>For those individuals released on bail prior to final disposition</u>

Today we see an expansion in the traditional use of bail to allow those not financially able to provide bond the chance to be released on a "recognizance bond." Halfway houses may serve an important role in this expansion.

A standard requirement for recognizance bonding is that the individual have roots in the community. The halfway house may be able to serve those without community ties to make them eligible for recognizance bonding. The halfway house can provide supervision, as well as treatment services, to those individuals who would otherwise be forced to wait in jail for their final disposition.

8. <u>For diversion from the criminal justice system</u>

A possible future use of halfway houses is the diversion of problem individuals who are now forced into the criminal justice system (chronic alcoholic, drug abuser, or victimless crime offenders). Halfway houses, as well as public health facilities, can be utilized to divert and treat a substantial number of these individuals.

All eight Ohio halfway house systems have parolees and probationers as clients. Several of the houses also contract with the United States Bureau of Prisons to provide services to federal pre-releasees. The houses generally have some offenders with special problems (drug or alcohol), and one of the eight houses specializes in treatment of alcoholics.

Ohio houses also often have residents who may not have come to the house as a requirement of a supervisory agency; these people are designated "self referrals." They may have previously been (or may still be) parolees or probationers, but have not been required to reside in the house. These are individuals who realize that they need the help of a halfway house, and come to the house on their own volition to seek assistance.

In 1971, Ohio enacted a furlough statute. This allows the Ohio Adult Parole Authority to release prisoners to a community treatment center prior to the date they would ordinarily have been paroled. The individual can only be released for purposes of employment, vocational training, educational programs, or other programs designated by the Director of the Department of Rehabilitation and Correction. When an individual is released under the furlough program he must be confined for periods of time when he is not actually working at his approved employment or engaged in vocational training or other educational programs. Such confinement must be in a suitable facility designated by the Adult Parole Authority. Since the inception of the law, Ohio halfway houses have housed about 80 percent of all persons receiving furlough.[12]

An important policy issue which the evaluation will address is the type of resident with which halfway houses can be most effective. The outcome of all residents have been analyzed and attempts have been made to determine resident factors significantly related to success or failure. Resident factors that have a significant effect on outcome can then be used to develop recommendations for future policy.

While several program evaluations identify program effectiveness, many do not lend adequate information to the policy-making effort. In this specific evaluation, the project will attempt to go beyond measures of outcome to identify factors which affect outcome and need to be considered in future program policy determination.

It can be argued and is assumed that program evaluations can be a valuable tool in the policy-making process, but have been either veglected or inadequately utilized in the past. Evaluation procedures that increase the potential for and utility in policy making will be examined, and the problems most often cited for non-utilization of evaluations are critiqued.

Hypotheses

Before presenting the hypotheses to be examined in this study, several assumptions and research questions should be stated. Regarding the use of evaluations as instruments for policy making, the following assumptions have been made and will be further addressed below:

1. Correctional administrators fail to utilize program evaluation extensively or effectively in the policy-making process.

2. There are several relevant reasons for the lack of utilization of policy analyses in policy making, including the inability of the evaluator to construct his findings in a manner conducive to use by the policy maker.

3. There are adjustments that can be made by the evaluator to allow his work to be a useful policy-making instrument.

4. Policy making in corrections can be facilitated by consideration of relevant information supplied by program evaluations.

These assumptions are addressed below in both conducting a study of Ohio halfway houses and analyzing the utilization of the evaluation for the decision making and future planning of halfway house services.

The hypotheses to be tested in the evaluation include the following:

1. There will be no difference in outcome between residents assigned to halfway houses and those comparison group cases not utilizing the services of a halfway house.

2. Within halfway house residents, there will be no differences in outcome measures. The different classifications of halfway house residents cannot be differentiated in outcome.
3. Changes in policy will have no effect on the future loads of halfway houses or the costs to the correctional system.

Summary

The American correctional system is currently undergoing radical changes in philosophy. Originally, criminals received corporal or capital punishment administered by and within their own communities. About 1790, incarceration became the standard disposition for criminal offenders. During the 1970's, the trend is reverting to keeping the offender in the community--providing him counseling, support, and guidance, while encouraging him to develop more acceptable living patterns.

Although this change in policy has come about as a result of the perceived inhumanity and ineffectiveness of institutions, community-based corrections as an alternative has not been throughly evaluated to determine the alleged effectiveness, nor had the decision to implement community programs come about from a rational or synoptic approach of considering all alternatives and choosing among them in relation to their preferred consequences.

It appears that this development or decision resulted from what March and Simon would call "the satisfying model," in which a policy is accepted (without searching for the maximizing policy) if it satisfies objectives previously determined by the policy maker.[13] This decision-making model, which is more behavioral than normative, is often used and widely accepted. Nonetheless, whether one argues the merits of the rational or satisfying decision-making model, there is certainly agreement on the need for evaluation of program policy, and feeding results back to the planning function.

It is the assumption and emphasis of this study that evaluations in the correctional area should be used as instruments for policy making. The assumption is made that, in the field of corrections, evaluations are not extensively or adequately used for this purpose, due both to a lack of trust or concern by the administrator and to the inability of the researcher to provide relevant and pragmatic information for the policy process.

This problem is significant and cannot be lightly dismissed. Without adequate evaluations and a resultant improvement in programming, the trend toward community-based corrections could fail to attain desired goals and encounter the same problems of ineffectiveness which have led decision makers away from the institution as the basic treatment modality for offenders. Community corrections could thus be seen in history as a short-run "fad" which proved no more effective in reducing crime than institutional treatment. The resultant philosophy would, of course, be to revert to the use of institutions, where the public would at least be "safe from convicted criminals." In other words, more stress would then be placed on an incapacitation rather than reintegration philosophy for corrections.

The field of program evaluation in criminal justice has been cluttered with non-useful and misleading evaluations which reflect inconclusive evidence of program effectiveness. Although inappropriate evaluations per se cannot be blamed totally for program ineffectiveness, the insensitivity of evaluations to the issues in outcome measurement and inability to provide useful information for policy making have not contributed to the improvement of community programs.

To illustrate the possible use of a correctional program evaluation, an evaluation of Ohio adult halfway houses has been undertaken. Halfway houses act as supervised community placements for parolees, probationers, furloughees, and pre-releasees--offering individual and group counseling, a therapeutic environment, and basic needs to the offender in his attempt to reintegrate himself into society.

The evaluation will utilize what, it could be argued, is a more realistic measure of outcome than the traditional operational

15

definition of recidivism. From outcome analyses, house program and individual offender characteristics will be examined to determine their significance in relation to post-treatment behavior.

The evaluation will entail not only a simple statement of program effectiveness, but will also attempt to identify and recommend necessary changes in policy for the improvement of the overall program. Alternative methods for handling offenders are considered and their effects on present policy described.

FOOTNOTES - CHAPTER I

1. President's Commission on Law Enforcement and Administration of Justice, Task Force Report: Corrections (Washington, D.C.: U.S. Government Printing Office, 1967), p. 7.

2. President's Commission, Task Force Report: Corrections, p.13.

3. John M. McCartt and Thomas J. Mangogna, Guidelines and Standards for Halfway Houses and Community Treatment Centers (Washington, D.C.: U.S. Government Printing Office, 1973), pp. 33-34.

4. Alice M. Rivlin, Systematic Thinking for Social Action (Washington, D.C.: The Brookings Institute, 1971), pp. 91-93.

5. David J. Rothman, The Discovery of the Asylum (Boston: Little Brown and Company, 1971), p. 62.

6. Quoted in Edwin Powers, "Halfway Houses: An Historical Perspective," American Journal of Correction 21 (July-August 1959): 22.

7. President's Commission, Task Force Report: Corrections, p.27.

8. President's Commission, Task Force Report: Corrections, p.60.

9. Dennis C. Sullivan, Larry J. Seigel, and Todd Clear, "The Halfway House, Ten Years Later: Reappraisal of Correctional Innovation," Canadian Journal of Criminology and Corrections 16 (April 1974): 188-197.

10. These are listed as eight "systems" because some of the listings have multiple facilities which service various types of ex-offenders.

11. McCartt and Mangogna, Guidelines and Standards, pp. 22-29.

12. Ohio Adult Parole Authority, Furlough Program Guidelines (Columbus: Ohio Department of Rehabilitation and Correction, 1973), p. 1.

13. James G. March and Herbert A. Simon, Organizations (New York: John Wiley, 1958), p. 136.

CHAPTER II

METHODOLOGICAL CONCERNS IN PROGRAM EVALUATION

As argued in Chapter I, it is asserted that evaluations should be an integral element in policy making for developing community correctional programs. Although more evaluations of programs are presently being completed than at any other time in the history of modern corrections, it is believed that many of these evaluations have little, if any, effect in the determination of program policy.

Both evaluators and program administrators are in part responsible for the ineffective use of evaluations as a feedback mechanism for policy making. The administrator must become more dedicated to assisting in the evaluative effort and utilizing results. However, unless the evaluation is designed for practical utilization by the administrator, he is not likely to become overly committed to the effort.

There are two important issues to be considered in the development of an evaluative design: (1) the ability of the administrator to utilize the results of the evaluation in the determination of policy, and (2) constraints on the evaluator in controlling the experiment. The evaluative design must lead to practical solutions of problems or information that is useful for program planning. This is a sometimes complex task, requiring a special effort by both the evaluator and administrator to extract valid information from often loosely-structured programs.

The second consideration is also important, since a rigorous controlled experiment may conflict with attempts to provide practical information and recommendations. It is fairly easy to develop a truly experimental evaluative design; however, there are generally several limitations in the implementation of such a design for social programs. Difficulties in random selection of control and experimental groups often times force evaluators to rely on other than the experimental design.

The question can therefore be formulated: "What methodological considerations need to be examined in order to design evaluations that lead to relevant and realistic results useful to the policy-making process?" This chapter identified such concerns and recommends possible approaches to answering the above question. Initially, the conceptualization of program objectives must be examined. After measurable and realistic objectives have been identified, it is possible to develop the evaluative design, define outcome measures, and consider utilization of evaluative information for program development and policy making.

Defining Program Objectives

The first step in the evaluation of a program is to determine program objectives. Program effectiveness should be judged through a measurement of its ability to accomplish prescribed objectives. Simon contends that to measure organizational effectiveness, it is essential to look at a set of goals.[1] McCartt and Mangogna further discuss the importance of goals in evaluation.

> Evaluation must measure the outcome of the program and services in relation to the agency's stated prupose and goals. Program and service effectiveness must be measured by recognized evaluation techniques, and when possible, by formal research.[2]

Problematic in the evaluation of many social programs is a lack of clear, specific, and measurable objectives. This problem is further compounded by the fact that social programs often have many sub-goals which must be defined and evaluated. It is therefore important for the evaluator to collaborate with program administrators in defining realistic program objectives that can be measured in tests of program effectiveness.

Evaluators are often initially provided very general and nebulous goal statements. Nebulous goal statements are often times the result of a "quick and dirty" goal formulation process during the writing of applications for funding. Since agencies appear to perceive (perhaps accurately) a need to state far-reaching goals in order to be funded, a goal setting process may result in statements

19

of unrealistic and unreachable goals. Goal statements may not be relevant for evaluative purposes, and if used as a basis of measurement, could result in a determination of program ineffectiveness. When faced with unrealistic goal statements, the evaluator should encourage the administrator to develop additional program objectives which provide an actual description of program operations.

The best example of stating unrealistic program goals may well be found in criminal justice programs. Goal statements often consist of a promise to reduce crime or recidivism by a certain percentage. Although recidivism and crime reduction are measurable goals, they are often totally unrealistic and if utilized would indicate the ineffectiveness of the program in reaching its stated goals.

Whether any criminal justice program can result in a reduction of crime or recidivism is even questionable. Gerald M. Caplan, Director of the National Institute of Law Enforcement and Criminal Justice (the research agency of the Law Enforcement Assistance Administration), in an interview by the Los Angeles Times, stated that crime "is largely--though not completely--beyond the proper span of government, at least in a democratic society, to control."[3]

Following Caplan's lead, program administrators should consider the possibility that they cannot reduce crime and recidivism. Perhaps these sacred goals should be regarded as unreachable and, although they may continue to be ideally sought, should not be used as the basis for evaluating program effectiveness.

When a reduction in crime or recidivism is listed as a program goal, evaluators should encourage administrators to list other, more realistic sub-goals for evaluative purposes. Then, even though the prime objective of a reduction in crime may not be reached, the program may be found to have been quite effective in accomplishing sub-goals.

There are times in which a program may be extremely effective in accomplishing sub-goals, yet have no effect on reducing crime or recidivism. Within criminal justice, and more specifically correctional philosophy, there are several accepted and perhaps supported theories regarding the relationship of certain variables and the reduction of crime or recidivism. For instance, almost all criminologists would agree that keeping an ex-offender employed will contribute to a reduction in his likelihood to recidivate. Glaser, in his study of the federal prison and parole system, stated that "unemployment may be among the principal causal factors in recidivism of adult male offenders."[4]

However, the exact extent to which employment affects an ex-offender's chance for success is not know, essentially because the significance of this variable will differ in each individual case. Administrators may decide that assisting ex-offenders to procure and retain employment will reduce recidivism, and thus strive to develop a program to accomplish this objective. If the program does assist clients in procuring and retaining a job but there is no reduction in recidivism, the program should not be judged as ineffective. If administrators had initially realized their objective was to provide job procurement services and defined objectives in these terms, the program would be "successful," regardless of the recidivism rate of the clientele. If the provision of jobs does not lead to a reduction in recidivism, either the original hypothesis is simplistic or there are too many extraneous and confounding variables that washed out the effect of the job procurement program.

The important element is for program administrators to define measurable and realistic program goals. For social service agencies, goal statements should be developed around the accomplishment of providing needed services, rather than around sacred or traditional measures of program success. An individual program may not be able to reduce recidivism, but this should not deter administrators from providing services which theoretically contribute to reducing recidivism.

After administrators have recognized the importance of identifying measurable and realistic objectives, the process of establishing goals must be determined. It is not sufficient to define goals that will be useful only to an evaluation. However, the evaluative process can be extremely helpful to the administrator merely because it forces him to develop goal and objective statements which have utility in program management.

Since program objectives are useful both to the evaluation and management of programs, the process of establishing objectives is important. There appear to be three methodologies for setting of objectives. These are (1) individual initiative, (2) committee planning, and (3) management by objectives.[5]

Setting objectives by individual initiative is illustrated by referring decisions to one individual who, presumably, has determined the objectives for the group and retains the power to make decisions on the basis of those objectives. Many criminal justice programs u-ilize this goal-setting process. The program director may thus be forced to develop program goals without previously prescribed guidelines. Although some capable directors may set realistic and measurable goals, problems can still result if the decision-maker has not explicitly ennunciated goals to lower level staff. Also, staff may not be committed to accomplishing objectives which they had no part in setting.

In the committee planning approach, a group of people work together, hold dialogue, read, consult with experts, and finally produce a prose statement which gives a description of the desired ends. The committee planning approach is advantageous in that it involves persons throughout the organization. However, the outcome of this process is frequently highly value-laden, and objectives are often vague. This approach may be an acceptable way for a board of trustees to develop a philosophy or statement of purpose for an agency; however, operational objectives need to be more specific and workable in order to contribute to the overall program philosophy.

Management by objectives can be viewed both as a philosophy of management and a method for accomplishing it. Explicit objectives are set within an organization by a formal process that involves a flow of discussion both upward and downward through the organizational hierarchy. The upward and downward discussion involved in management by objectives allows optimum input by all staff members in goal setting. When this vertical discussion is completed, a significant number of individuals have participated in setting objectives, and there should be consistency among them. This process also offers an approach for satisfying, in part, the esteem need and needs for self-actualization by members of program staff.

Discussions among participants in the goal setting process should not be limited to simple statements of goal preferences, but should include structuring interrelationships among objectives levels. The development of interrelations leads to an ordering of objectives, perhaps in terms of priority but, more importantly, also in terms of a presentation of objectives as they contribute to other objectives levels. This ordering provides a structure for operations in terms of outlining activities that need to be completed to accomplish related objectives.

One method of presenting program objectives for this purpose is the objectives hierarchy. An objectives hierarchy is an ordering and arrangement of program objectives in a manner showing relationships among objectives. Thus an objectives hierarchy has at least two aspects. First, it presents a vertical structure of objectives with broadly stated objectives at the top, and specific measurable objectives at the bottom. Secondly, it shows vertical and horizontal interdependencies of objectives within the structure.

As stated above, it is important that an evaluation be structured so as to be useful for administrators in improving the management of a program. Even in the formulative stages of an evaluation, techniques for defining evaluative goals are also useful for program management. Chapter III illustrates a process of eliciting goal statements from persons associated with halfway house programs, and the development of an objective hierarchy to be used for both the evaluation and management of these programs.

Designing the Evaluative Structure

After program goals have been identified and enunciated, the evaluator must develop an appropriate evaluative design for testing program effectiveness. The design must be structured to allow the effected experimental treatment to be measured and program effectiveness tested. This necessitates operationally defining and examining the experimental variable, while controlling for the effect of extraneous variables.

Control over or for extraneous variables frequently complicates the evaluative design, especially in a social program.[6] Laboratory experimentation will generally allow the researcher to hold all other variables constant, changing only the variable to be tested, and measuring the effect of these changes. However, when examining social programs, it is unethical and often impossible to hold constant all other variables which affect the outcome. Social scientists must therefore select groups in which they assume the effect of these variables is equally distributed, or control for their occurrence by statistical techniques or methods.

The classic design for evaluations is the true experimental design, a model using both an experimental and control group randomly selected from the target population. Weiss writes, "The essential requirement for the true experiment is the randomized assignment of people to programs."[7] Utilizing random assignment to experimental and control groups assumes any uncontrolled variables will affect the groups equally, and any difference in outcome can therefore be attributed to the experimental variable.

Evaluators in criminal justice programs should attempt to utilize a true experimental design whenever it is possible to do so without altering operational program practices to the extent that the evaluated program bears little resemblance to the program that will operate after completion of the evaluation. The evaluator therefore needs to be well versed in the powers and restrictions involved in utilizing a true experimental design.

Campbell and Stanley discuss three true experimental designs: the pretest-posttest control group design, the Solomon four-group design, and the posttest-only control group design.[8] The pretest-posttest control group design in which equivalent groups are achieved by randomization can be symbolically diagrammed:

$$R_E \; O_1 \; X \; O_2$$

$$R_C \; O_3 \quad O_4$$

The "R" indicates that all cases are first randomly divided into experimental and control groups. "O_1" and "O_3" represent the pretest of the groups prior to the experimental group receiving the treatment "X" to be tested. "O_2" and "O_4" then represent the posttest administered both groups. This design allows for comparisons of O_1/O_3, O_1/O_2 and O_3/O_4, and O_2/O_4 to determine program effectiveness. In terms of power, this design controls well for internal validity, but there remains a lack of robustness in control for certain sources of external validity.[9]

A second true experimental design is the Solomon four-group design. While the pretest-posttest control design may be used more frequently, the Solomon four-group design is more powerful, and methodologically carries higher prestige, representing the "first explicit consideration of external validity factors."[10] The symbollic design is as follows:

$$R_E \; O_1 \; X \; O_2$$

$$R_C \; O_3 \quad O_4$$

$$R_E \quad \; X \; O_5$$

$$R_C \quad \quad O_6$$

By paralleling the pretest-posttest design with a control and experimental group lacking the pretest, the main effects of both the interaction of testing as well as "X" are determinable.[11]

The third true experimental design is the posttest-only control group design. Its form is as follows:

$$R_E \; X \; O_1$$

$$R_C \; X \; O_2$$

The major reason for a pretest is to determine if the groups are in fact equal after random selection. However, the underlying assumption of randomization would lead to this conclusion without the pretest. Campbell and Stanley argue that this design is "true experimental," since the randomized selection would rule out any initial biases between groups, and the pretest "is not actually essential to true experimental designs."[12]

Even though the true experimental design is acknowledged as being the most powerful in producing valid results, there are several problems inherent in the utilization of these designs for social analysis. Weiss discussed several possible problems in attempting to utilize true experimental designs:

1. There may be absolutely no extra people to serve as controls; the program serves everybody eligible and interested.
2. Practitioners generally want to assign people to treatment based on their need, as judged by the practitioners' professional knowledge and experience.
3. On occasion, control groups become contaminated because the members associate with people in the experimental program and learn what they have been doing. Controls may also be provided the same type of treatment by other agencies.[13]

Guba and Stufflebeam also find fault in the experimental model because:

1. It requires holding the program constant rather than facilitating its continual improvement.
2. It is useful for making decisions only after a project has run a full cycle and not during its planning and implementation.
3. It tries to control too many conditions, making the program so aseptic that it is ungeneralizable to the real world.[14]

Another problem (and a major source of resistance to controlled experimentation in correctional programs) is that "the treatment to be tested, if more lenient than traditional practice, appears to endanger the public or to conflict with governmental goals other than changing those ajudged deviant."[15] Recently, this was found to be true when suggesting an experimental design for a program in which normally incarcerated offenders would be treated in the community.[16] State parole officials would agree to random selection of offenders to be returned to prison and those to be assigned to supervised community residential centers. However, the suggestion that another randomly selected group be retained in the community with no supervision prompted the comment that the parole authority was mandated to protect society and could not responsibly withdraw supervision from any group.

Although problems inherent in the use of true experimental designs do merit consideration, these should not totally deter the use of true experimental designs. It would appear that the major dilemma for criminal justice evaluation is the practitioner's emphasis on non-random assignment, with assignment to treatment groups by client need. However, Campbell suggests that random assignment is much more possible than many would suspect.[17]

One example of a situation in which administrators wanted to assign persons as subjects in their treatment program according to client needs exemplifies Campbell's argument. In matching volunteers to probationers, evaluative personnel were able to convince program staff of the merit of random assignment to control and experimental groups. Post-evaluative curiosity led evaluators to isolate the outcome of those identified clients who were previously defined by staff as needing the program services and were subsequently randomly assigned to the experimental group. The need of these clients for assistance was accurately perceived; their outcome scores were lower than the average in the experimental group. Assignment of clients to the program solely in terms of need would have made the experimental group a more difficult clientele, probably resulting in very negative indicators of program effectiveness, and leading to questionable conclusions.

However, there are valid situations in which evaluators of criminal justice programs are unable to utilize true experimental designs. Evaluators are often asked to conduct an ex post facto study to determine program effectiveness. In this situation, there is no possibility to randomize groups, and the evaluator must resort to the use of a quasi-experimental design.

Quasi-experimental designs do not satisfy the strict

methodological requirements of the experimental design, but can be quite useful and powerful when the researcher is aware of the specific variables for which the chosen design does not control. Weiss contends:

> Quasi-experiments have the advantage of being practical when conditions prevent true experimentation. But they are in no sense just sloppy experiments. They have a form and logic of their own. Recognizing in advance what they do and do not control for, and the misinterpretation of results that are possible, allows the evaluator to draw conclusions carefully. Quasi-experiments, in their terms, require the same rigor as do experimental designs.[18]

Campbell and Stanley discuss ten quasi-experimental designs, some utilizing groups other than the experimental for comparison purposes, and some which do not.[19]

A frequently utilized and practical design for criminal justice evaluations is the non-equivalent control group design. In the non-equivalent control group design, there is no random assignment to experimental and control groups, but groups with similar characteristics are used as controls. Non-randomized controls are generally referred to as "comparison groups."

Evaluators utilize various procedures in attempting to select comparison groups that are as similar as possible to the experimental group. Quite often, evaluators attempt to develop a comparison group by matching procedures, either pairing individual members of the experimental and comparison groups on selected measures, or matching the entire experimental group to a similar group based on the same selected factors or parameters.

However, there are several problems associated with matching groups for evaluative purposes. It is difficult to select the most relevant characteristics on which to match subjects. In correctional philosophy, there is little consensus on the most important factors related to outcome. Since matching factors vary in importance from case to case, it is difficult to select the most relevant factors. It may also be difficult to match individuals on several dimensions. Individual cases may perforce be eliminated from the experimental group due to the inability to match when several matching factors are required.

An alternative approach is the use of predictive methods to develop comparable groups. Although prediction methods in criminal justice are generally used in selection and placement, several authors have noted that they may be most useful in the evaluation of treatment programs.[20] Rather than developing similar comparison groups, the evaluator uses prediction methods to provide a measure of expected performance based on the individual characteristics of the experimental group, and compares "actual" to "expected" outcome.

Prediction models are based on the theory that by studying parameters such as demographic variables, previous offense records, test scores, or previous experiences, an individual's future behavior can be predicted. Comparisons of expected performance with actual performance allow a measure of success of the experimental group based on a comparison within that group. In this sense, the subject's expected performance is his own control.

Some authors argue that a predictive model may not validly be used to predict a single individual's behavior. Hayner lists five reasons parole boards lag in the use of prediction tables: (1) sensitivity to public opinion, (2) desire to encourage constructive use of prison time, (3) firm belief in the uniqueness of each case, (4) frustration of intelligent selection for parole because of legal or traditional restrictions, and (5) reactions to the prediction devices themselves.[21]

However, these arguments against the use of prediction do not appear relevant when using predictive methods as evaluative tools. The use of prediction as an evaluative tool is not an attempt to predict a single individual's behavior, but rather to determine a group's expected behavior for comparative purposes.

A statistical technique infrequently used due to its complexity and tedious calculation, but with relevant application to social research, is analysis of covariance. Analysis of covariance is seen to combine the most important factors in matching and prediction. With this technique, the evaluator can select the matching variables to be used as covariates, and is also provided the attributes of prediction in that these covariates are weighted according to their importance to outcome.

Analysis of covariance involves two basic steps. Initially, the selected control variables are correlated against the sets of outcome scores to determine their relationship to outcome. After determination of the effect of each control variable on outcome, means of outcome scores are adjusted to reflect the effect of the control variables. In effect, control variables are correlated with original or "raw" outcome scores to determine their effect on the score, each control variable weighting is applied to the raw score to predict what this score would be if the groups were equal in regards to the control variables, and the raw scores are then adjusted to reflect an equalization of the groups and allow comparison of the adjusted scores.[22]

Analysis of covariance has several advantages to matching an experimental group to a comparison group of similar characteristics. Matching forces a choice of factors to be matched, while each parameter is weighted equally. In utilizing analysis of covariance, the evaluator can select as covariates the parameters on which the two groups differ, and allow the technique to adjust those variables weighted according to their effect on outcome.

Chapter IV illustrates the use of analysis of covariance in developing a comparison group and determining the effectiveness of halfway house treatment in assisting ex-offenders. This technique is herein proposed as a useful tool for evaluators when unable to randomly assign individuals to control and experimental groups.

Measures of Outcome

In the selection of outcome measures to test program effectiveness, several factors should be considered. Glaser notes that:

> No definition of success can be useful unless methods of measuring its attainment are sufficiently precise, valid, and reliable to warrant confidence that they improve the quality of knowledge available for guiding policy makers.[23]

The evaluator should, of course, select evaluative outcome measures based on program objectives. As previously stated, program objectives should be realistic so that measures of outcome can relate program success to the possible accomplishment of stated objectives.

Throughout the last 50 years in corrections, evaluators have relied on and principally utilized recidivism rates to measure the success of a program. Recidivism is usually measured in terms of rearrest, reconviction, or reimprisonment. Evaluations of correctional programs utilizing these indicators have failed to conclusively identify programs that reduce recidivism. Negative findings have not been limited to evaluations of prison programs;[24] community-based correctional programs also have yet to be found an effective alternative.[25]

A crucial policy question is: "Is the failure of corrections to correct due entirely to ineffective programs?" The answer to this question is difficult to comprehend in all certainty. Findings of program ineffectiveness can in part be due to the insensitivity of recidivism as a measure of outcome. It seems unreasonable to argue that the experienced and talented persons who have attempted to develop programs for reducing recidivism could have failed so miserably.

The deficiencies of recidivism as an outcome measure are important. One must consider if recidivism is a reasonable and valid indicator of an individual's re-entry into society. Recent victimization studies have indicated actual crime to be as much as five times higher than reported crime,[26] and one should be aware of the discrepancy between those who commit further crimes and those who are arrested, convicted, and incarcerated for their offenses.

However, this discretion will probably continue to plague the criminal justice system; no individual outcome measure can be completely valid if it relies on official records or court statistics. Self-reporting measures of outcome would alleviate the reliance upon official statistics for recording behavior; however, it is generally both difficult and expensive to conduct self-reporting studies. If the assumption were made that discrepancies between actual behavior and official records of behavior is consistent and has a constant (if perhaps unknown) relationship, comparisons between groups based on official records should still be valid.

A problem exists when attempting to compare program evaluations. Lacking a standard definition of recidivism, evaluators resort to the utilization of several levels of recidivism. Recidivism is broadly defined as a relapse to crime or deviant behavior; however, among studies this definition can vary from arrest to reimprisonment. Without standardized definitions of outcome measures, it is impossible to relate evaluative data to other, similar programs.

Perhaps the most serious problem in the use of recidivism as an outcome measure is the forced dichotomous choice; recidivism classifies each offender as either a "success" or a "failure," rather than grading them on a continuous scale to measure "progress." Glaser emphasizes this point:

> Any measure of the success of a people-changing effort which fails to take into account variations in the degree to which a goal has been obtained, and instead classifies all the research subjects as either successes or failures, is thereby limited in its sensitivity as an index of variations in the effectiveness of alternative programs and policies.[27]

It seems reasonable that people-changing programs cannot substantially change people within a relatively short period of time. Changes will be incremental and hopefully in the direction the program emphasizes. This gradual process has been acknowledged in correctional philosophy, even though most professionals continue to judge a program's success by dichotomous measures of recidivism. Realizing that the reintegrative process is gradual, evaluators can no longer be permitted to use dichotomous measures of success and failure in determining program effectiveness.

Another problem in the use of recidivism indicators is that they are a negative measurement of criminal actions, and do not consider positive behavior or "adjustment." Therefore, a treatment program would not receive credit for developing acceptable living patterns within offender clients unless criminal behavior were totally eliminated. The reintegrative model mandates an

additional measure of positive behavior. Since correctional programs seek to replace negative-valued behavior with positive
behavior, outcome measures should include both types of indicators,
sensitive enough to detect slighter progressive changes in the
individual.

An offender is probably never a complete "success" or
"failure." Even if an individual was a failure in the traditional
sense--in that he had been rearrested or reimprisoned, he may have
made significant strides toward success. For instance, if an
offender has been accustomed to supporting himself 100 percent by
criminal activity, and now works full time at a job and only
receives 50 percent of his income from criminal activity, could he
not be judged a partial success? And, although he may be rearrested
or reimprisoned, is he a complete failure? Outcome measures must
be sufficiently sensitive to detect and enhance minor movements in
behavior.

Correctional philosophy appears to be shifting from the rehabilitative to the reintegrative model. O'Leary and Duffee have
summarized four models of correctional policy as presented in
Figure 1.[28]

FIGURE 1
MODELS OF CORRECTIONAL POLICIES

		Emphasis on the Community	
		Low	High
Emphasis on the Offender	High	Rehabilitation (Identification Focus)	Reintegration (Internalization Focus)
	Low	Restraint (Organizational Focus)	Reform (Compliance Focus)

The rehabilitative model emphasizes supportive control and punishment as therapy; the atmosphere sought approaches that of a
hospital. Diagnosis and treatment are part of the vocabulary used
in labeling the offender as "sick" rather than "criminal." After

treatment, the offender is expected to be released as a "well" person who will be successful in adapting to societal living. In this model, the prison is a remote, independent unit free from contamination, where the practitioners work with inmates in individualized programs.[29]

On the other hand, the reintegrative model provides the offender alternatives of behavior while in the community rather than isolated in a prison. O'Leary and Duffee have written:

> Emphasis on the community does not mean simply a stress on maintaining its values but in promoting changes as well within its institutional structure to provide opportunities for offenders and reduce systematic discrimination because of economic and cultural variances.[30]

Reintegration is not perceived as an overnight change, but the gradual adoption of socially-acceptable behavior as this behavior is practiced and reinforced. John Conrad, in describing the reintegrative model, has written: "Where this model is applied, the process will be the internalization of community standards."[31]

The development and utilization of a continuous scale to include both positive and criminal behavior will be discussed below. This outcome measure ("relative adjustment") is also based on the offender's personal characteristics and, in that sense, compares him only with his own expected behavior. The relative adjustment measure of outcome should remedy many of the proglems in the use of traditional outcome measures described above.

Developing Policy From Evaluations

Evaluations of criminal justice programs do not influence policy decisions or facilitate program planning, due to several factors. Quite often, the inability of evaluations to affect policy-making is in part due to insensitive outcome measures which furnish inconclusive evidence regarding program effectiveness. What might be called the "no effect syndrome" has plagued numerous evaluations of reintegrative programs which have been found to have no significant effect on the outcome of their clients.

The use of recidivism rates as an outcome measure and the

resultant forced dichotomy is more likely to cause errors in validity than a continuous scale allowing for graduated levels between success and failure. Utilizing dichotomous measures does not allow for the rejection of the null hypothesis, but instead leads to a type II error--the inability to reject the null hypothesis--which is however, less damaging than introducing a false positive finding. This often results in a lack of conclusive evidence as to program effectiveness, and an inability for administrators to determine any pattern of success or failure among clients.

For instance, practitioners often attempt to identify program graduates which they feel will be successes or failures based on their performance in the program. However, outcome studies have indicated that these practitioners are unable to predict client outcome from their program performance.[32] It is reasonable to ask if program performance is a poor indicator of outcome, or if the outcome measure used by the practitioner to predict behavior is perhaps invalid. When a dichotomous measure of outcome is used, an ex-offender who does not work, is supported by relatives, and does not attempt to help himself is classified a "success" if he does not commit a new crime. Yet most persons would not label the above behavior "successful." Due to the false success indicators, programs which practitioners intuitively (and perhaps correctly) feel are effective may be shown by evaluations to be ineffective.

Evaluation can also fail to have an impact on policy making when it is not possible to relate outcome results to categories of residents or segments of program operations. After determining outcome measures, the evaluator, on an ex post facto basis, should attempt to search for relationships between categories of clients' success (or failure) and program operations. For example, if successful in this endeavor, the evaluator might conclude that younger clients receive the most benefit from the vocational segment of the experimental program.

Analysis of covariance, on the other hand, can be a valuable tool for isolating categories of residents who have benefited or can potentially benefit from the program. Several categories of residents (in parameters such as age, type of offense, level of education) are examined individually in Chapter V. Utilizing the analysis of covariance technique, each resident category is examined in relation to the comparison group. This can pinpoint categories of residents who receive benefit from the program.

In examining outcomes for various categories of residents, the evaluator must not simply conduct comparisons between outcome scores within the experimental group. It is a simple process to divide the experimental group into various categories, compare mean outcome scores, and conclude that the group with the highest mean outcome score received the most benefit from the program. However, because a certain category of client has the highest mean score, it may not have received as much benefit as a group with a lower mean score.

When the analysis of covariance is used for examination of differences in benefit to client categories, the evaluator is provided "adjusted" actual and predicted (comparison group) scores. The difference in these scores can be attributed to participation in the program, and provides an actual measure of benefit received from participation. In determining the benefit received, the difference in the adjusted scores is more important than the raw mean scores. It is possible that although a particular category of client has a lower mean score than other categories, such clients have received more benefit from the program. The evaluator and program administrator are now provided with an indication of categories of clients with whom they can be most effective.

In addition to providing administrators indications of types of clients with which the program can be effective, an evaluation can also provide projections for future trends or policy implications resulting from present operations or changes in operations. Extremely valuable information for program administrators is a projection of population loads and service costs for future years.

Chapter VI includes a mathematical representation of the processing of offenders through the Ohio correctional system, to include halfway houses. The representation provides load and cost data for all incarceration and post-incarceration states. Models developed can be useful for manipulating loads resulting from simulated policy changes, and discovering long range implications of such policy changes of the various states included in the model.

The development of evaluative techniques used to provide information for the future is extremely important in criminal justice programs. Evaluations should not limit their outlook to the past, determining the effect of the studied program in an ex post facto manner, but should build on the ex post facto analysis with techniques for discovering information useful to administrators in determining policy and program projections for the future. Chapter V and VI illustrate possible techniques for increasing the benefit of evaluations to the receivers of the information.

FOOTNOTES - CHAPTER II

1. Herbert A. Simon, "On the Concept of Organizational Goals," Administrative Science Quarterly 9 (June 1964): 1-22.

2. John M. McCartt and Thomas J. Mangogna, Guidelines and Standards for Halfway Houses and Community Treatment Centers (Washington, D.C.: U.S. Government Printing Office, 1973), p. 33.

3. Los Angeles Times interview with Gerald M. Caplan, as reported in Criminal Justice Digest 2 (December 1974): 1-3.

4. Daniel Glaser, The Effectiveness of a Prison and Parole System (Indianapolis: Bobbs-Merrill, 1964), p. 32.

5. John N. Warfield, An Assault on Complexity (Columbus: Battelle Memorial Institute, 1973), p. 8-1.

6. For more information on intervening variables, see: Carol H. Weiss, Evaluative Research: Methods of Assessing Program Effectiveness (Englewood Cliffs, N.J.: Prentice Hall, Inc., 1972), pp. 45-53.

7. Weiss, Evaluative Research, p. 67.

8. Donald T. Campbell and Julian C. Stanley, Experimental and Quasi-Experimental Designs for Research (Chicago: Rand McNally and Company, 1972), p. 13.

9. Sources of internal validity are: (1) history, (2) maturation, (3) testing, (4) instrumentation, (5) statistical regression, (6) selection biases, (7) experimental morality, and (8) selection-maturation interaction. Sources of external validity are: (9) reactive or interactive effect of testing, (10) interactive effects of selection biases and the experimental variable, (11) reactive effects of experimental arrangements, and (12) multiple treatment inferences. For a detailed explanation of internal and external validity, see: Campbell and Stanley, Designs for Research, pp. 5-6.

10. R.L. Solomon, "An Extension of Control Group Design," Psychological Bulletin 46 (1949): 137-150.

11. Campbell and Stanley, Designs for Research, p. 24.

12. Campbell and Stanley, Designs for Research, p. 25.

13. Weiss, Evaluative Research, p. 63.

14. Egon G. Guba and Daniel L. Stufflebeam, "Evaluation: The Process of Stimulating, Aiding, and Abetting Insightful ction," address delivered at 2nd National Symposium for Professors of Educational Research, Columbus, Ohio, November 21, 1968.

15. Glaser, Routinizing Evaluation, p. 67.

16. The author was involved in developing an evaluative design to test the effectiveness of treatment centers as an alternative to reimprisoning parole violators. The discussions of suggested evaluative designs took place with the evaluation team and correctional officials.

17. Donald T. Campbell, "Reform as Experiments," American Psychologist 24 (1969): 409-429.

18. Weiss, Evaluative Research, pp. 67-68.

19. For a detailed examination of these designs, see: Campbell and Stanley, Designs for Research, pp. 34-64.

20. See: Herman Mannheim and Leslie T. Wilkins, Prediction Methods in Relation to Borstal Training (London: Her Majesty's Stationery Office, 1955); Don M. Gottfredson, "The Practical Application of Research," Canadian Journal of Corrections 5 (October 1963): 212-228; Don M. Gottfredson, Kelly B. Ballard, and J.A. Bonds, Base Expectancy: California Institution for Women (Sacramento: Institute for the Study of Crime and Delinquency, and California Department of Corrections, 1962); Don M. Gottfredson and J.A. Bonds, A Manual for Intake Base Expectancy Scoring (Sacramento: California Department of Corrections, 1961); Don M. Gottfredson and Kelly B. Ballard, "Testing Prison and Parole Decisions," 1966.

21. Norman S. Hayner, "Why Do Parole Boards Lag in the Use of Prediction Scores?" Pacific Sociological Review 1 (Fall 1958): 73-76.

22. Charles Logan, "Evaluative Research in Crime and Delinquency," Journal of Criminal Law, Criminology, and Police Science 63 (September 1972): 378-387.

23. Daniel Glaser, Routinizing Evaluation: Getting Feedback on Effectiveness of Crime and Delinquency Programs (Washington, D.C.: Department of Health, Education, and Welfare, 1973), p. 16.

24. Robert Martinson, "What Works?--Questions and Answers About Prison Reform," Public Interest, no. 35 (Spring 1974): 22-25.

25. Dennis C. Sullivan, Larry J. Seigel, and Todd Clear, "The Halfway House, Ten Years Later: Reappraisal of Correctional Innovation," Canadian Journal of Criminology and Corrections 16 (April 1974): 188-197.

26. National Criminal Justice Information and Statistics Service, Criminal Victimization in the United States (Washington, D.C.: U.S. Department of Justice, 1974), pp. 1-8.

27. Glaser, _Routinizing Evaluation_, p. 22.

28. For detailed description of these four models, see: Vincent
    O'Leary and David Duffee, "Correctional Policy--A Classifi-
    cation of Goals Designed for Change," _Crime and Delinquency_
    17 (October 1971): 378-383.

29. O'Leary and Duffee, "Correctional Policy," p. 380.

30. O'Leary and Duffee, "Correctional Policy," p. 382.

31. John P. Conrad, "Reintegration: Practice in Search of Theory,"
    in Reintegration of the Offender into the Community
    (Washington, D.C.: National Institute of Law Enforcement and
    Criminal Justice, 1973), p. 13.

32. Stuart J. Miller, "Post-Institutional Adjustment of 443
    Consecutive TICO Releases" (Ph.D. dissertation, The Ohio State
    University, 1971), pp. 83-99.

CHAPTER III

ESTABLISHING GOALS AND OBJECTIVES OF OHIO
HALFWAY HOUSES FOR EVALUATIVE PURPOSES

It is difficult to identify a set of common goals for all community treatment centers; there seem to be no clearly defined or commonly accepted goals for such centers. Often times, statements of purpose or goals restate the rationale that the offender may be "better" treated in the community, where the foundations of his problems lie and without the deleterious effects of isolation from society. Although much effort is currently being devoted to standards and goals throughout the criminal justice system, proclamations regarding halfway house goals are sparse.

The variability of residential centers prohibits promulgation of a single prescription of goals to fit the various types of houses. The type of client to be serviced must therefore be a principal concern in the determination of program goals.

Statements of general goals may be extracted from the conceptual framework for residential centers as expressed by the Corrections Task Force of the President's Commission on Law Enforcement and Administration of Justice:

> The general underlying premise for the new directions in corrections is that crime and delinquency are symptoms of failures and disorganization of the community as well as of individual offenders. In particular these failures are seen as depriving offenders of contact with the institutions (of society) that are basically responsible for assuring the developing of law-abiding conduct . . . .
> The task of corrections therefore includes building or rebuilding solid ties between the offender and the community, integrating or reintegrating the offender into community life--restoring family ties, obtaining employment and education, securing in the larger sense a place for the offender in the routine functioning of society . . . . This requires not only efforts directed toward changing the individual offender, but also mobilization and change of the community and its institutions.[1]

These statements reflect the correctional emphasis of aiding the offender in his resocialization into the community. The residential center should provide a programmed and supervised transition to productive community living. However, programs need to be flexible, geared specifically to goal-oriented diagnoses of cases and directed toward each offender's achievement of progressive self-sufficiency in the community. The residential center per se cannot maintain all necessary resource services in-house, and frequently acts as the focal point or liaison for the ex-offender and other community agencies or institutions.

Although the varying nature of residential centers is not conducive to applying a single set of prescribed goals to all houses, this does not negate the need for carefully developing planned goals for the management of individual programs. After development of goals, they should be disseminated throughout local criminal justice agencies, so these latter agencies can formulate a realistic idea of what each halfway house can do for offenders.

Ohio Halfway House Goals

To determine present operational halfway house goals, house directors and staff, state parole officers, and state probation officers were asked what they think to be the goals of halfway houses in Ohio, and what are appropriate goals for houses providing services to clients. While all halfway house directors and staff responded to questionnaires, this was not true with all parole and probation officers. Table 1 represents the return rate for these groups.

TABLE 1

PAROLE AND PROBATION OFFICER RETURN RATES

	Parole Officers	Probation Officers
Number of questionnaires administered	140	75
Number of usable questionnaires returned	97	36
Return rate	69%	48%

The thirty goals listed by the 133 responding halfway house directors and staff, parole officers, and probation officers are presented in Table 2, ranked in order of the total number of persons mentioning each as an objective of the halfway house.

Data in Table 3 illustrate the actual number of responses in each group. Parole and probation officer responses are further divided into groups having or not having had clients supervised in a halfway house.

TABLE 2

HALFWAY HOUSE GOALS

1. To provide vital needs (food, shelter) in a therapeutic environment.	(88)
2. To facilitate reintegration of the ex-offender.	(71)
3. To provide employment counseling and services.	(69)
4. To develop an individualized program around the resident's needs.	(51)
5. To rehabilitate individuals.	(27)
6. To provide for the safety of society.	(27)
7. To assist with special problems (alcohol, drugs).	(24)
8. To assist in goal planning of residents.	(21)
9. To instill personal responsibility within residents.	(21)
10. To improve resident self-concept.	(18)
11. To provide educational services and guidance.	(14)
12. To offer a community alternative to incarceration.	(13)
13. To utilize community resources.	(13)
14. To prevent future criminal acts.	(12)
15. To rebuild family ties.	(8)
16. To provide for resident's spiritual needs.	(8)
17. To sensitize and educate the community to corrections.	(7)
18. To induce behavior modification.	(7)
19. To provide financial counseling and assistance.	(7)
20. To instill self-discipline within residents.	(6)
21. To provide peer group counseling.	(6)
22. To de-institutionalize ex-offenders.	(6)
23. To supervise and control residents.	(4)
24. To provide guidance in interpersonal relationships.	(4)
25. To provide aftercare and follow-up services.	(4)
26. To serve as a focal point for community and resident interaction.	(4)
27. To train future correctional staff.	(2)
28. To provide alternatives to criminal action.	(2)
29. To provide constructive leisure activities.	(2)
30. To provide crisis-intervention services.	(1)

A simple presentation of these listings is not enough to assist halfway house directors in managing their operations. However, there are several relevant issues that can be inferred from this ranking. It is also possible to construct an objectives hierarchy which can be of assistance in the management process.

TABLE 3

HALFWAY HOUSE GOALS BY RESPONDENT GROUPS

Goal Number	Halfway House Directors (N=10)	Halfway House Staff (N=31)	Parole Officers (N=97)		Probation Officers (N=36)	
			Clients in Houses	No Clients in Houses	Clients in Houses	No Client in Houses
1	7	7	26	30	5	13
2	4	17	24	20	3	3
3	6	16	24	16	2	5
4	7	6	19	15	4	10
5	2	5	5	5	2	8
6	2	1	7	6	3	8
7	2	0	8	6	2	6
8	1	5	8	5	1	1
9	1	9	4	4	1	2
10	3	8	4	2	0	1
11	2	2	6	1	1	2
12	3	3	3	1	0	3
13	6	1	1	1	2	2
14	2	3	2	1	2	2
15	3	2	1	0	0	2
16	1	7	0	0	0	0
17	4	1	1	0	0	1
18	1	6	0	0	0	0
19	3	2	0	0	1	1
20	0	1	4	1	0	0
21	1	0	2	3	0	0
22	2	4	0	0	0	0
23	0	0	1	0	2	1
24	0	2	2	0	0	0
25	1	0	1	1	0	1
26	3	0	1	0	0	0
27	1	1	0	0	0	0
28	2	0	0	0	0	0
29	2	0	0	0	0	0
30	1	0	0	0	0	0
Total	83	140	154	118	31	72

Congruence Among Goals

This section includes an examination of how well halfway house goals have been disseminated to other coordinating agencies, and the degree of concurrence in relation to stated goals. As stated before, it is important for various criminal justice agencies to have a knowledge of the goals of halfway houses.

In addition to asking respondents about the goals of halfway houses, respondents were also asked what the goals should be if different than they were presently. Using a Spearman rank order correlation, the degree of association was so strong that the null hypothesis (stating that there was no correlation between what the goals are and what they should be) was rejected at the .05 level of significance.

Although there was substantial agreement between actual and desired goals, there was a noticeable difference in both parole and probation officers' responses in regard to Objective 23, control of residents. Officers felt control should be considered a more important goal than is presently perceived, which is an expected response. The major halfway house foci are toward benefiting the resident, while working toward developing a total treatment milieu in the house. Traditionally, however, parole and probation officers have been primarily charged with custody and secondarily with treatment. This difference in basic orientation may explain the difference in perceived importance of control of residnets as a house goal.

Both house directors and staff have a significant amount of interaction with residents, and have the discretion to implement objectives they feel are important. Since goal statements by directors and staff appear to realistically represent actual implemented house objectives, it is important that there be a high degree of correlation between their responses.

Assuming the null hypothesis of no correlation between directors and staff ratings, the Spearman rank correlation coefficient value indicated rejection of the null hypothesis at the .05 level. Therefore, there is significant agreement between directors and staff on perceptions of goals.

Parole and probation officers had initially been divided into respondents with clients in the houses and those without clients in the houses. However, groups' responses (using the Spearman r) were found to be correlated at the .01 level of significance. Scores were therefore combined into all parole officers and all probation officers. Table 4 indicates the combination of statements of goals into three groups.

In testing for correlation between responses of groups, it was found that responses by halfway house personnel and by all parole officers were correlated; results on the Spearman test were found to be significant at the .05 level. This indicates a substantial agreement between the perceived house goals as expressed by halfway house personnel and parole officers.

There were only two items on which the two group's responses widely differed. In contrast with halfway house personnel, parole officers rated assistance with alcohol and drug problems of higher importance. Parole officers are perhaps more likely to perceive the use of halfway houses for multi-problemed individuals needing more intensive supervision than they can provide.

Probation officers' responses as to perceived goal statements were even more highly correlated with responses of house personnel (Spearman correlation coefficient value was so great the null hypothesis was rejected at the .01 level of significance). Probation officer responses differed from house personnel on some of the same items. In contrast to halfway house staff, probation officers more frequently perceived house goals of assistance with drug and alcohol problems, and control of residents.

This analysis indicates that among groups surveyed, there is general agreement regarding the perceived goals of Ohio halfway houses. This is an important finding and issue, since persons responsible for referring clients to halfway houses must have a knowledge of house philosophy and operations in dealing with the ex-offender.

TABLE 4

HALFWAY HOUSE GOALS BY COMBINED RESPONDENT GROUPS

Goal Number	Halfway House Personnel (N=41)	Parole Officers (N=97)	Probation Officers (N=36)
1	14	56	18
2	21	44	6
3	22	40	7
4	13	34	14
5	7	10	10
6	3	13	11
7	2	14	8
8	6	13	2
9	10	8	3
10	11	6	1
11	4	7	3
12	6	4	3
13	7	2	4
14	5	3	4
15	5	1	2
16	8	0	0
17	5	5	1
18	7	0	0
19	5	0	2
20	1	5	0
21	1	5	0
22	6	0	0
23	0	1	3
24	2	2	0
25	1	2	1
26	3	1	0
27	2	0	0
28	2	0	0
29	2	0	0
30	1	0	0
Total	223	272	103

Objectives Hierarchy

One method of operationalizing program objectives is the development of an objectives hierarchy, an ordering of program objectives

in a manner which shows the relationships among the objectives.
An objectives hierarchy has a least two aspects. First, it presents a vertical structure of objectives with broadly stated
objectives at the top and specific measurable objectives at the
bottom. Secondly, it shows vertical and horizontal interdependencies of objectives within the structure.[2] The basic structure
of an objectives hierarchy follows:

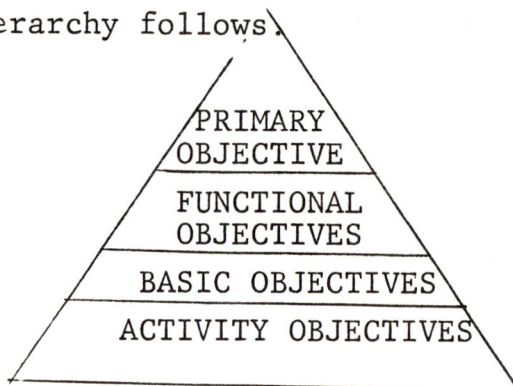

```
                    /\
                   /  \
                  /PRIMARY\
                 /OBJECTIVE\
                /_____\
               / FUNCTIONAL  \
              /  OBJECTIVES    \
             /_____\
            /   BASIC OBJECTIVES  \
           /_____\
          /   ACTIVITY OBJECTIVES    \
         /_____\
```

A primary objective is the purpose or overall philosophy of a
program. It can be viewed as a composite of the values and beliefs
upon which a program is based. It also embraces the major areas
for which the program can assume responsibility.

Functional objectives reflect the critical operations required
for achieving the primary objective. Usually broad in scope, functional objectives are directed toward the establishment of
operational guidelines and/or constraints. Although more specific
than the overall purpose, they are often not quantifiable.

Basic objectives, on the other hand, are designed to be both
specific and measurable. This lower level of objectives contributes to achievement of the functional objectives above them, while
providing a basis for measuring the degree of success involved in
the accomplishment of functional objectives.

Activity objectives are specific services or activities to be
provided to clients. These objectives should describe the details
of actions to be completed to accomplish the basic objectives, and
are the specific activity elements accomplished with direct services
to clients.

Examples of halfway house objectives on the primary, functional,
basic, and activity levels are as follows:

48

<u>Primary objective</u>:	To facilitate reintegration of an individual into the community while preserving the safety of that community.
<u>Functional objective</u>:	To provide individualized programming to alter behavior or residents.
<u>Basic objective</u>:	To assist with special problem areas of the resident.
<u>Activity objective</u>:	The resident will receive ten house of one-to-one counseling on job procurement within the first three weeks of residency.

As can be seen, the lower objectives on the hierarchy construct a foundation for those above them. The activity objectives are a means to accomplish the basic objectives; accomplishment of basic objectives leads to functional objective completion; and the primary objective of the organization is accomplished only when all the lower level objectives have been fulfilled.

Using the thirty objectives as stated by halfway house personnel and parole and probation officers, an objectives hierarchy has been constructed. Although placement of objectives in the hierarchy is perhaps arbitrary and may differ from house to house, it does present the technique of construction. Simply, the process of constructing the hierarchy provides administrators with thought-provoking questions such as: "What are our house objectives, how do they relate to one another, and what objectives need to be achieved to accomplish a higher level objective?"

The possible distribution of objectives into a hierarchy using the thirty halfway house objectives would be as follows.

Primary objective

The primary objective is a combination of two stated objectives.
  . To facilitate reintegration of the individual into the community while providing for the safety of citizens.

Functional objectives

Functional objectives are divided into two areas. The first are those objectives which address the needs of residents as consumers of services of the social welfare services of the halfway house.

  . To develop an individualized program around the
    resident's needs in order to alter behavior.

Secondly, there are those objectives which address the needs of
the criminal justice system and its responsibilities.

  . To assist the criminal justice system in the
    rehabilitation of offenders.

These two, of course, are not mutually exclusive. However, the
first functional objective focuses on the offender's needs while
the second objective considers the mandates of the criminal justice system.

Basic objectives

Basic objectives contribute to the achievement of objectives
above them. Although they are presented as contributing to functional objectives either focusing on offender needs or criminal
justice mandates, some may be classified as both.

Resident basic objectives

  . To provide vital needs (food, shelter) in a thera-
    peutic environment.
  . To de-institutionalize ex-offenders.
  . To assist in goal planning of residents.
  . To instill personal responsibility within residents.
  . To improve resident's self-concept.

Criminal justice system basic objectives

  . To sensitize and educate the community toward
    corrections.
  . To offer a community alternative to incarceration.
  . To prevent future criminal acts.
  . To train future correctional staff.

Activity objectives

Activity objectives are services or activities which make up
the basis for accomplishing overall program objectives. Activity
objectives can also be divided into two sections: those which
address the needs of residents and those which address the need of

the criminal justice system. Although some objectives reflect the needs of both residents and the criminal justice system, the following have been categorized as mainly addressing the needs of residents.

Resident activity objectives

- To utilize community resources.
- To provide employment counseling and services.
- To assist with special problems (alcohol, drugs).
- To provide educational services and guidance.
- To rebuild family ties.
- To provide for residents' spiritual needs.
- To provide for financial counseling and assistance.
- To provide peer group counseling.
- To provide guidance in interpersonal relationships.
- To provide constructive leisure activities.

Objectives below have been categorized as generally addressing the needs of the criminal justice system.

Criminal justice system activity objectives

- To serve as a focal point for community and resident interaction.
- To provide aftercare and follow-up services.
- To instill self-discipline among residents.
- To supervise and control residents.
- To provide alternatives to criminal action.
- To provide crisis-intervention services.

Objectives hierarchy for Ohio halfway houses

All four levels of objectives are presented in an objectives hierarchy to illustrate both the vertical and horizontal interdependencies of the objectives (see Figure 2).

Management and the Objectives Hierarchy

"The primary functions of management are planning, organizing, communicating, and evaluating."[3] Halfway house directors, as any

FACILITATE REINTEGRATION AND PROTECT SOCIETY

ASSIST CJS IN OFFENDER REHABILITATION

INDIVIDUALIZED PROGRAM DESIGNED TO ALTER BEHAVIOR

TRAIN FUTURE CORRECTIONS WORKERS

PREVENT FUTURE CRIMINAL ACTS

SUPERVISE AND CONTROL RESIDENTS

OFFER COMMUNITY ALTERNATIVE TO INCARCERATION

PROVIDE AFTERCARE AND FOLLOW-UP SERVICES

CRISIS INTERVENTION

SENSITIZE AND EDUCATE COMMUNITY

SERVE AS FOCAL POINT FOR INTERACTION

INSTILL SELF-DISCIPLINE

PROVIDE ALTERNATIVES TO CRIMINAL ACTION

PROVIDE VITAL NEEDS

DE-INSTITUTIONALIZE OFFENDERS

ASSIST IN GOAL PLANNING

INSTILL PERSONAL RESPONSIBILITY

IMPROVE SELF-CONCEPT

UTILIZE COMMUNITY RESOURCES

PROVIDE EDUCATIONAL SERVICES AND GUIDANCE

REBUILD FAMILY TIES

PROVIDE FOR SPIRITUAL NEEDS

PROVIDE FINANCIAL COUNSELING AND GUIDANCE

PROVIDE CONSTRUCTIVE LEISURE ACTIVITIES

ASSIST WITH SPECIAL PROBLEMS

PROVIDE PEER GROUP COUNSELING

PROVIDE EMPLOYMENT COUNSELING

PROVIDE GUIDANCE IN INTER-PERSONAL RELATIONSHIPS

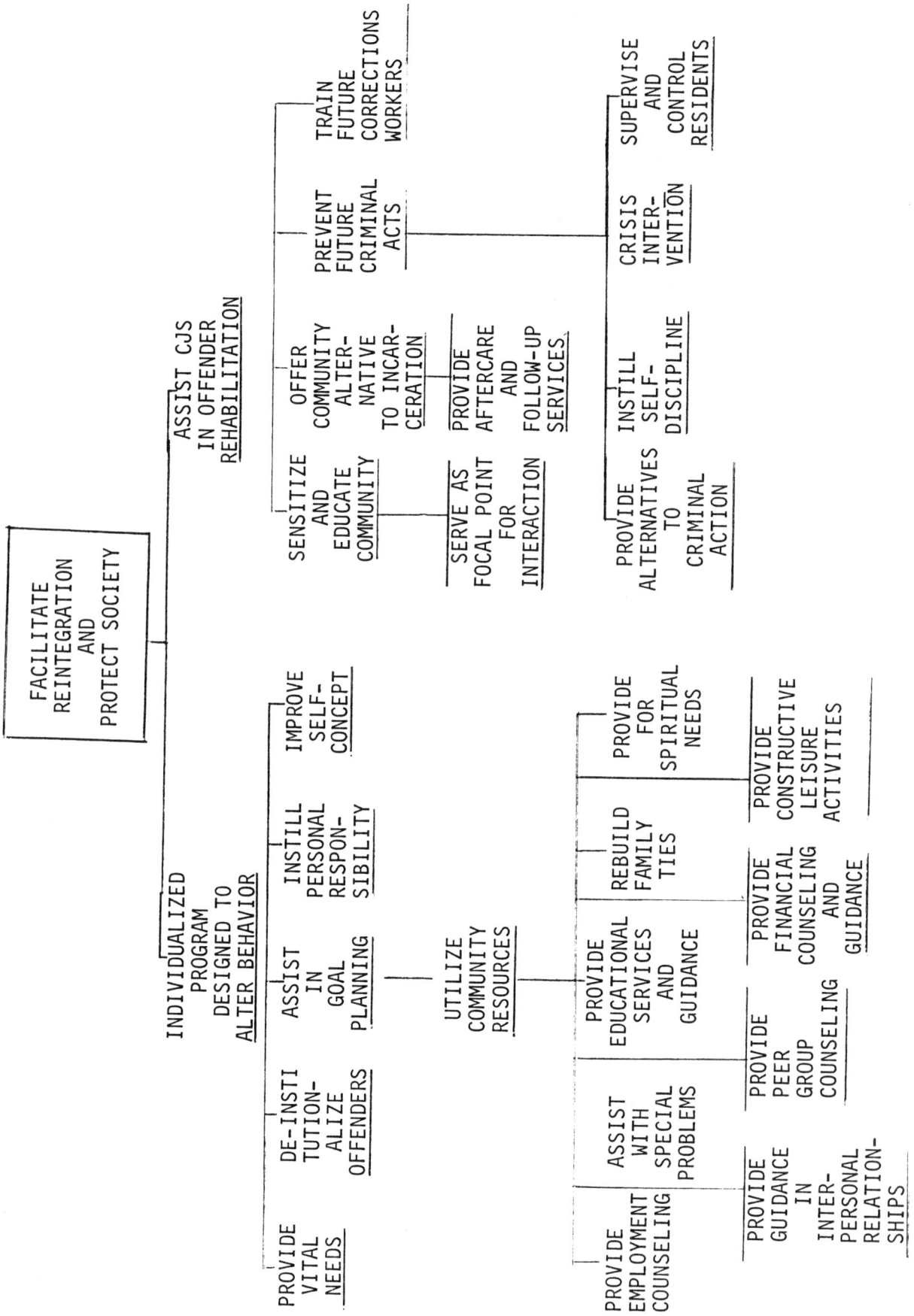

FIGURE 2: HALFWAY HOUSE OBJECTIVES HIERARCHY

52

other administrators, are faced with each of these problems in the management of their houses. The house director is therefore concerned with how an objectives hierarchy can help with management problems. The use of an objectives hierarchy or objectives tree certainly is not a total solution for management problems. It can, however, be useful in adding structure and organization to many phases of management.

Management concepts such as "management by objectives" and "participative management" may also not be the definitive answer for halfway houses. Management by objectives requires a rather stable organization,[4] and many halfway houses are still undergoing "growing pains." However, this does not preclude use of the several principles entailed in both of these theories. In fact, during the initial stages of program development, an objectives tree and participation throughout all staff levels may be extremely beneficial to house management.

Justification for utilizing objectives systematically through an objectives hierarchy to structure halfway house program objectives is offered by O'Leary and Duffee:

> A stress on goals shifts the focus away from an exclusive concern with the offender and his characteristics toward a view that places him within a correctional system continuously accomodating itself to a larger social order.[5]

The use of the objectives process

Setting objectives by use of the management by objectives method has at least two positive features. First, it includes staff in the objectives-setting process and in the accomplishment of objectives consistent throughout the organization. Second, it allows for the assignment of "owners" of objectives responsible for their accomplishment.

After objectives have been established and agreed upon through the use of a participative process, staff may be assigned primary responsibility for accomplishing specific objectives. An instructive example is the assignment of objective responsibility by matching the objective hierarchy with the organizational hierarchy. For instance, the board of trustees is responsible for the accomplishment of primary objectives. Meanwhile, they hold the director responsible for accomplishment of functional objectives-- those operations which contribute to achievement of the primary objective.

The assistant director is responsible for accomplishing basic objectives. He systematically assigns activity objectives to various staff members. For instance, a staff member may be responsible for employment counseling, another for group counseling, and another for recreation. Matching the objectives hierarchy to the organizational hierarchy allows assignment of specific responsibility for each objective level.

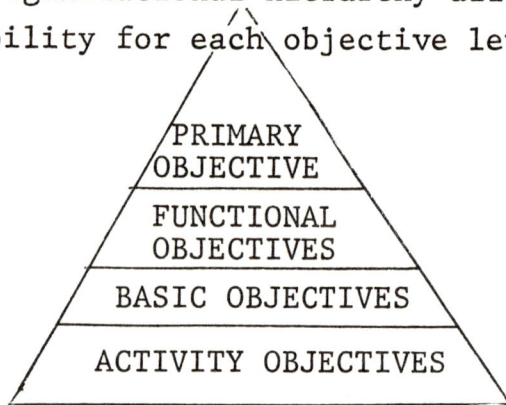

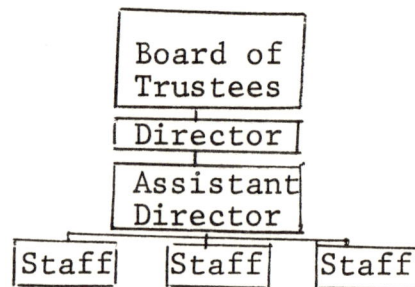

Planning

Systematic planning of social welfare programs is imperative for efficient management. In systematic planning, the total problem is analyzed and alternative solutions examined. Some basic steps to systematic planning are presented below:

- . Define the problem and the planning task. This includes preliminary research to describe target populations and their needs, and identifying those individuals who will assist in the planning.
- . Formulate policies on the basis of value analysis of alternative solutions (deciding what ought to be).
- . Assess operational resources and constraints, including the source of clientele, funding, legislative factors, and community preferences.
- . Consider priorities, including the extent of funding necessary, and identify what services have to be established to meet program objectives.
- . Develop a program structure that includes such activities as administration, manpower assignment, budgeting, and feedback for policy review.
- . Establish specific projects with long and short range objectives.

. Design a system of reporting and evaluating, and provide formal feedback to the planning system.[6]

These steps can be utilized with the objectives hierarchy to establish planning directives. Using this format, an example is presented of planning using the objectives hierarchy for a volunteer program for court probationers. The problem defined in the primary phase is the deleterious effects of incarceration, and the need to use probation as an alternative. It is assumed that offender reintegration is more effective when attempted in the non-incarcerated context. The primary objective would then be as follows:

. To reintegrate probationers.

At the second or functional level, assessment of resources and constraints, and consideration of policy and guidelines are completed. With probation caseloads rising and probation officers unable to offer satisfactory personal services, a volunteer program to assist with probation supervision would appear beneficial. The program would attempt to accomplish two functional goals:

. Provide personal services designed around the individual needs of the probationer.

. Encourage community acceptance of criminal offenders (probationers).

Moving down the hierarchy to the basic level, program areas are selected to meet the needs of the program. Using the present example, basic objectives are chosen that will lead to fulfilling the needs of the problem defined in the primary level:

. Improve self-esteem and general attitude.

. Lower criminal behavior.

. Develop acceptable living patterns in the community.

. Educate volunteers.

. Sensitize the community.

Projects and services to implement the program are next considered at the activity level; these are the actual services to be provided. In this example, this list would include the following:

. Provide the probationer with a friend.

. Assist with employment problems.

. Offer educational counseling and guidance.

. Aid the probationer with socialization problems.

. Develop training sessions for volunteers.

. Encourage personal contact between the volunteer and probationer.

. Encourage volunteers to discuss their program involvement with others.

. Recruit volunteers.

. Conduct a public relations campaign.

This process presents a logical method for planning the operations of new programs, while stressing planning from the problem and needs statement "down," or planning what needs to be accomplished at each level to accomplish the level above it.

However, planning in criminal justice and other social welfare programs is often the exact opposite process. Planners will sometimes start with a problem, and immediately develop services they feel will resolve the problem, without carefully examining intermediate objectives and alternative solutions. Other times, planners may begin to implement services without considering the primary objective.

The objectives hierarchy is perhaps most useful in the deliberation of "cause and effect" relationships between levels of objectives in the program design. Many social welfare agencies are lacking in organized planning, and should consider this method of organizing objectives as a minimal requirement for effective planning. In the development of an evaluative design, the evaluator should encourage the administrator to list objectives rationally in an objectives hierarchy. Not only will this enhance the evaluative effort, but it will also be a useful tool for planning and managing program operations.

56

FOOTNOTES - CHAPTER III

1. President's Commission on Law Enforcement and Administration of Justice, Task Force Report: Corrections (Washington, D.C.: U.S. Government Printing Office, 1967), p. 7.

2. Robin J. Milstead, "The Use of an Objectives Hierarchy in Planning, Operating, and Evaluating Halfway House Programs" (M.S.W. paper, The Ohio State University, 1973).

3. Willaim D. Hitt, "Management by Objectives in Educational Systems" (memorandum).

4. John N. Warfield and J. Douglas Hill, A Unified Systems Engineering Concept (Columbus: Battelle Office of Corporate Communications, 1972), p. 76.

5. Vincent O'Leary and David Duffee, "Correctional Policy--A Classification of Goals Designed for Change," Crime and Delinquency 17 (October 1971): 373-386.

6. J. Ann George and R.J. Milstead, "A Systems Approach to Planning, Service Delivery, and Evaluation of Alcoholism Programs," paper presented at National Conference of Alcohol and Drug Problems Association, Minnesota, 1973.

CHAPTER IV

DEVELOPING SENSITIVE OUTCOME MEASURES
FOR EVALUATION

A major component of any criminal justice program evaluation is the determination of program effectiveness based in part on a measurement of client outcome. Relevent problems in both the development of an evaluative design which would include a valid comparison group, and the utilization of outcome measures which are sensitive to incremental changes in client behavior have been discussed in Chapter II. This chapter provides an illustration of several techniques designed to remedy these problems and obtain results useful for policy analysis.

The first hypothesis to be tested in this analysis requires the use of an instrument to measure the outcome of residents of Ohio halfway houses and a comparison group. To repeat the null hypothesis stated in Chapter I:

> There will be no difference in outcome between residents
> assigned to halfway houses and those comparison group
> cases not utilizing the services of a halfway house.

This hypothesis will be tested utilizing an outcome measure developed and detailed in this chapter.

The target group in this example includes residents of the eight adult halfway house systems (ten houses) in Ohio. Outcome data covering a twelve-month period have been collected and utilized in the development of measures of program success. This example further illustrates an evaluation of community treatment centers (halfway houses) utilizing techniques for determining the effectiveness of houses in supplementing traditional aftercare services and assisting the ex-offender in his reintegration to the community.

Experimental and Comparison Groups

The experimental group of halfway house clients is made up of 236 subjects including parolees (144), probationers (31), and federal offenders on pre-release status (61). The comparison group includes 404 parolees released from Ohio institutions during 1973. Initially, a random selection of all inmates released on parole during the first six months of 1973 was chosen; all parolees utilizing halfway houses were then excluded, leaving for the comparison group 404 parolees who had never utilized halfway house services. A demographic description of both the halfway house and comparison groups is presented as Appendix A.

The assignment of clients to halfway houses based on their perceived need for services has made it impossible to develop a true experimental design utilizing random assignment into control or experimental groups. Therefore, a quasi-experimental design was chosen and efforts made to control statistically for selection biases.

The selection problem is common to evaluators of criminal justice programs. Unless a program has developed as a demonstration project with a rigorous evaluative design essential to the effort, the evaluator will be forced to sacrifice experimental design for realistic program operations. If an offender were to have community ties and would not benefit from the intensive treatment of a halfway house, there is no need to incur the expense of halfway house placement in addition to the costs of parole or probation. Although random assignment to the houses and to the control group would permit a true experimental design, clients would be assigned to houses who would not ordinarily be provided services. Therefore, the evaluation would not test the actual contributions of halfway houses to the correctional process.

To identify and control for the acknowledged selection process, comparisons were made between the experimental and comparison groups on demographic data, criminal records, employment history, and previous alcohol or drug use (see Appendix A for a comparative analysis of groups). Using z-scores to test for significant differences between group characteristics and utilizing the .05 probability level, the following statistically significant differences were found between the groups:

1. The comparison group has a higher percentage of Blacks.
2. The halfway house group has a higher rate of juvenile delinquency.
3. The halfway house group was younger at the age of their first offense.
4. The halfway house group has twice as many prior offenses as the comparison group.
5. The halfway house group has more offenses as adults.
6. The halfway house group has more felony offenses.
7. There are more multiple offenders in the halfway house group.
8. There are more victimless crime offenders among the halfway house group.
9. The comparison group had previously been employed a higher percentage of their lives.
10. A higher percentage of the halfway house group has an identified drug problem.

Since there are significant and theoretically important differences between the halfway house experimental and the comparison groups, steps were taken to correct for the differences and permit comparisons of outcomes between groups. The dependent variable is the outcome indicators for the experimental and comparison groups. Several independent variables (the ten variables in which there was significant difference between the groups) were corrected to allow for a more valid comparison.

An analysis of covariance (as described in Chapter II) has been used to control for the ten independent variables. This technique measures the effect of the independent variables on the dependent variables, and statistically corrects for the difference and effect by calculation of adjusted outcome scores.

Relative Adjustment

Adequate and useful analysis of the outcome of community correctional programs has been very limited to date.[1] Since part of this condition is due to the insensitive indicators of outcome previously utilized, a new measure of outcome (founded on the reintegrative correctional philosophy) has been used. This measure, labeled relative adjustment (RA), is designed to be a more sensitive and realistic measure for determining program effectiveness and in applying the information to the policy-making process.

The relative adjustment model has two major components. The first component is a continuous outcome criterion. The index is continuous in order to alleviate the forced dichotomous distinctions of "success" and "failure." So as not to rely totally on negative or deviant behavior parameters, additional factors defined as "acceptable adjustment patterns" have also been included in a graduated scale of relative adjustment. The two scales are more sensitive to movement away from deviant behavior and toward acceptable behavior than are dichotomous outcome measures. Scores of positive and criminal behavior, when combined with the second component of RA (the utilization of analysis of covariance to correct for the relative differences in the groups), make up the "relative adjustment" outcome indicator utilized in this study.

Criminal Behavior Criteria

Although recidivism has been the most frequently used outcome criterion, several studies have utilized outcome measures of various degrees of seriousness of criminal behavior. Perhaps the most widely used is the Sellin-Wolfgang Index of Delinquency. This index, developed primarily for weighting the seriousness of juvenile delinquency, classifies specific delinquency events as to the involvement of property damage, theft of property, or personal injury.[2]

A second measure of criminal behavior is the Severity of Offense Scale developed and used by the Division of Research of the Youth Authority of the California Department of Corrections. Classifying offenses of apprehended youth, it scores the offense on a scale from "0" for no classifiable offense to "10" for those most severe offenses.[3]

Other studies have used various degrees of seriousness, basing the severity on the disposition rather than the offense. Gottfredson and Ballard used terms such as "major difficulty" and "minor difficulty" when classifying disposition.[4] Seiter used three dispositional levels of recidivism: arrest without charge; fined or sentenced to less than one year in jail; and sentenced to more than one year in prison.[5]

The recidivism index used in the present analysis is an ordinal ranking of severity of offenses as prescribed by the Ohio Criminal Code. The Code was developed after consultation with criminal justice experts and passed by the Ohio General Assembly; severity assignments are therefore assumed to be valid.

Recidivism measures are often based on the disposition of the offense; however, this can vary from court to court. Therefore, to maximize the reliability of the scale, only the offender's behavior (the actual offense) is considered. In utilizing the criminal behavior criterion, the offender is assigned a score based on the offense for which he has been found guilty or to which he has confessed. Although charges are often reduced from the actual offense in plea negotiating, this is assumed to occur equally between the groups and therefore should have minimal if any biasing effect on the outcome scores.

Since multiple offenses can occur during the twelve-month outcome analysis, the severity score for each offense is added. Therefore, it is theoretically possible for the offender to exceed the highest score on the scale. Also included in the scale are severity scores for technical parole or probation violations, and absconding or being declared a violator at large. Table 5 illustrates the severity categories and assigned scores for offenses.

Acceptable Behavior Criteria

A second element in the development of the total outcome criterion is the construction of a scale of "acceptable living patterns." The reintegrative correctional model does not assume a sudden change in behavior but rather movement away from criminal

TABLE 5

CRIMINAL BEHAVIOR SEVERITY INDEX

Offense Category	Assigned Severity Score
Aggravated murder	-11
Murder	-10
1st degree felony	-9
2nd degree felony	-8
3rd degree felony	-7
4th degree felony	-6
1st degree misdemeanor	-5
2nd degree misdemeanor	-4
3rd degree misdemeanor	-3
4th degree misdemeanor	-2
Violator at large	-1
Technical violation	-0.5

behavior and toward acceptable societal behavior. Therefore, an adjustment scale should be included as well as a recidivism scale. Several items generally considered to demonstrate "acceptable societal behavior" are presented in Table 6. These are not a complete list of success indicators, but merely selected factors which represent adjustment within the community.

A major emphasis of the adjustment scale is on work or educational stability, although self-improvement qualities, financial responsibility, parole or probation progress, and absence of critical incidents or illegal activities are also included. These items are somewhat discretionary and do not include all the qualities which could be defined as adjustment; however, each does suggest stability, responsibility, maturity, and a general order in a life style correlated with socially accepted patterns of behavior.

The construction of this adjustment scale was subjected to tests for validity and reliability. To validate the scale, a panel of experts was consulted. Numerous parole and probation officers, criminal justice researchers, former members of the Ohio Citizens' Task Force on Corrections, and other correctional professionals were consulted to determine items generally considered an indication

TABLE 6

ACCEPTABLE BEHAVIOR SCALE

Assigned Score	Adjustment Criterion
+1	Employed, enrolled in school or participating in training program for more than 50 percent of follow-up period.
+1	Held any one job (or continued in educational or vocational program) for more than six-month period during follow-up.
+1	Attained vertical mobility in employment, education, or vocational program. This could be raise in pay, promotion of status, movement to better job, or continuous progression through educational or vocational program.
+1	For last half of follow-up period, individual was self-supporting and supported any immediate family.
+1	Individual shows stability in residency. Either lived in same residence for more than six months or moved at suggestion or with agreement of supervising officer.
+1	Individual avoided any critical incidents that show instability, immaturity, or inability to solve problems in socially acceptable manner.
+1	Attainment of financial stability. This is indicated by individual living within means, opening bank accounts, or meeting debt payments.
+1	Participation in self-improvement programs. These could be vocational, educational, group counseling, alcohol or drug maintenance programs.
+1	No illegal activities on any available records during follow-up period.
+1	Individual making satisfactory progress through probation or parole periods. This could be movement downward in level of supervision or obtaining final release within reasonable period.

of acceptable adjustment.

To test the reliability of the scale, several individuals were asked to score an individual's adjustment criteria. This "debugging" exercise resulted in the formulation of certain standards for scoring and led to consistent scoring of the outcome index. These standardized scoring procedures are included in Appendix B.

Each adjustment criterion is weighted equally. Individuals receive a +1 score for each criterion on which they qualify according to the stated standards. The adjustment score is therefore the total number of criteria for which the individual has qualified, and can range from zero to ten.

The actual RA outcome criteria is then computed by considering both the criminal and acceptable behavior index scores. With this scale, an ex-offender's minor deviant behavior can be balanced with adjustment factors. Also, the ex-offender who refrains from illegal behavior but does nothing that otherwise qualifies as adjustment is not categorized as a total success, as he would be defined with traditional dichotomous recidivism measures. It is assumed that the RA score will provide a more realistic outcome criterion than had previously been available.

Relative Adjustment of Halfway House Residents

Utilizing analysis of covariance to correct for differences in the comparison and experimental groups, comparisons have been made between adjusted scores. Since groups are statistically comparable after adjustment of scores by analysis of covariance, differences between scores of the experimental and comparison groups can be interpreted as "predicted" and "actual" scores, as in the use of traditional prediction models. The actual acore is the halfway house group's adjusted score, while the predicted score is the comparison group adjusted score (the expected score if the halfway house group had not been exposed to house services). Since the groups are statistically comparable, differences in the adjusted scores represent the effect of the experimental variable (the halfway house experience).

Although the original experimental group totaled 236 persons, RA scores do not represent the outcome for all individuals. Outcome data was unavailable for approximately 10 percent of the cases, due to missing or incomplete records. However, there appeared to be no pattern for records being incomplete or missing, and the remaining sample for which records were available is assumed to be a valid representation of the total experimental group. The actual number of individuals included in the experimental group analysis is listed in the tables illustrating outcome scores. The comparison group has a sample size of 404 in every case.

Data in Table 7 illustrate the relative adjustment of the halfway house and comparison groups. It will be recalled that the relative adjustment score is a combination of the criminal behavior index and the acceptable behavior index. While scores for acceptable behavior have been assisned negative values. Therefore, the higher the relative adjustment score, the more favorable the adjustment outcome. The difference between the adjusted scores for the halfway house and comparison groups is indicated by the level of significance value. The null hypothesis will be rejected at the .05 level of significance.

TABLE 7

RELATIVE ADJUSTMENT SCORES

House Name	Half-way House Group N	Unadjusted Scores		Adjusted Scores		Level of Signi-ficance
		Half-way House	Compari-son	Half-way House	Compari-son	
Aggregate halfway house group	196	2.385	0.744	3.398	0.253	.01
Alvis	20	0.775	0.744	1.970	0.685	.98
Bridge	12	3.667	0.744	6.137	0.670	.23
Denton	32	2.375	0.744	4.177	0.601	.28
Fellowship	8	4.500	0.744	5.453	0.725	.21
Fresh Start	11	3.455	0.744	3.701	0.737	.29
Helping Hand	38	2.421	0.744	3.498	0.642	.23
Talbert McMillan	18	2.167	0.744	4.587	0.636	.47
Talbert Wesley	25	3.000	0.744	5.098	0.614	.18
Talbert for Women	17	1.559	0.744	3.732	0.652	.69
Vander Meulen	15	1.700	0.744	2.979	0.696	.66

The aggregate adjusted score for the halfway house group is 3.398, while the comparison group score is .0253; there is a significant difference between the scores of the two groups at the .01 level of significance. In terms of outcome, halfway house residents have significantly more favorable scores, suggesting that halfway houses are more effective at assisting ex-offenders in their reintegration to the community than the traditional modality of aftercare treatment. The null hypothesis of no difference between the outcome of halfway house residents and non-residents can be rejected. It is therefore reasonable to suggest that halfway houses are a more effective correctional modality for assisting offenders in the transition from the institution to the community, and as an alternative to incarceration for offenders placed under probation supervision.

These data also indicate the unadjusted and adjusted scores for each individual house, as well as the comparison group. In each case, the relative adjustment score for the halfway house group was higher than the score for the comparison group. Since the sample size of several houses is quite small (thus lowering the degrees of freedom for calculation of statistical significance), each separate house does not show a statistically significant difference when compared to the comparison group. When comparing the adjusted scores between the houses and the comparison group, one can note that several houses contribute positively to the significant difference between the aggregate halfway and the comparison group scores.

Within the components of the RA indicator, adjusted and unadjusted scores for the two groups on the criminal behavior severity index are presented in Table 8. The higher the score, the more severe and/or frequent the offense and therefore the less favorable the group score.

As can be seen from data in Table 8, there is a statistically significant difference between scores of the halfway house and comparison groups. The adjusted score for the halfway house group was -1.190, while the adjusted score for the comparison group was -3.665, a significant difference at the .001 level. Halfway house residents committed fewer and less severe offenses during the one-year outcome analysis than the comparison group. This suggests that halfway houses are effective in reducing the criminal behavior of residents.

TABLE 8

CRIMINAL BEHAVIOR SCORES[a]

| | Half-way House Group | Unadjusted Scores | | Adjusted Scores | | Level of Significance |
House Name		Half-way House	Comparison	Half-way House	Comparison	
Aggregate halfway house group	213	1.772	3.358	1.190	3.665	.001
Alvis	21	2.690	3.358	2.096	3.389	.64
Bridge	12	2.167	3.358	0.195	3.416	.54
Denton	37	1.730	3.358	0.460	3.474	.14
Fellowship	8	0.750	3.358	+0.225	3.377	.25
Fresh Start	14	0.786	3.358	0.685	3.361	.14
Helping Hand	40	1.650	3.358	0.912	3.431	.10
Talbert McMillan	22	1.273	3.358	+0.148	3.435	.13
Talbert Wesley	26	1.615	3.358	0.132	3.453	.17
Talbert for Women	18	1.861	3.358	+0.031	3.442	.33
Vander Meulen	15	2.967	3.358	1.981	3.394	.82

[a]Criminal behavior scores are all negative, except those marked +.

Again, scores for the individual houses did not attain a statistically significant level, perhaps due to the small numbers in the groups. However, even in the unadjusted score, residents of each halfway house scored more favorably than the comparison group, while the level of significance for several houses was near the acceptable .05 level. The statistical difference in aggregate criminal behavior scores allows for the reasonable conclusion that halfway houses are effective in reducing the frequency and lessening the severity of crime among ex-offenders.

The acceptable behavior scores have also been presented as a separate criterion of relative adjustment. It is now possible to examine the effect of halfway houses in assisting the ex-offender in developing acceptable behavior indicators. Data in Table 9 illustrate the scores for the comparison and halfway house groups in terms of positive behavior factors.

TABLE 9

ACCEPTABLE BEHAVIOR SCORES

| | Half-way House Group N | Unadjusted Scores | | Adjusted Scores | | Level of Signi- ficance |
House Name		Half-way House	Compari-son	Half-way House	Compari-son	
Aggregate halfway house group	196	4.311	4.101	4.708	3.909	.42
Alvis	20	3.600	4.101	4.199	4.072	.46
Bridge	12	5.833	4.101	6.332	4.087	.04
Denton	32	4.375	4.101	4.839	4.065	.61
Fellowship	8	5.250	4.101	5.228	4.102	.28
Fresh Start	11	4.455	4.101	4.896	4.089	.69
Helping Hand	38	4.158	4.101	4.526	4.067	.91
Talbert McMillan	18	3.722	4.101	4.419	4.070	.59
Talbert Wesley	25	3.680	4.101	5.258	4.066	.34
Talbert for Women	17	3.529	4.101	3.878	4.087	.43
Vander Meulen	15	4.667	4.101	4.960	4.091	.47

The aggregate and individual adjusted scores for halfway house residents are generally higher than the score for the adjusted comparison group. However, the difference in the aggregate scores for the groups is not statistically significant. Although this prevents rejecting the null hypothesis and drawing conclusions, the halfway house group has in general scored higher than the comparison group.

Examination of resident results in individual houses leads to some interesting findings. Residents of the Bridge, even with a very small sample, scored significantly higher on the adjustment index than the comparison group. Parenthetically, the bridge mades a concerted effort to locate jobs for residents and encourages them to stay employed.

On the other hand, Talbert for Women scores lower than the comparison group (which was 95 percent male). However, the lower positive adjustment score for women is not totally unexpected, since this index is heavily weighted with work and employment variables. Women ex-offenders may be married and have a family and, although adjusting well, may be fulfilling the more traditional female roles of staying at home caring for their families, rather than being employed in the community. This is a limitation of the RA indicator which future research may be designed to address.

Relative Adjustment Versus Recidivism

Relative adjustment data have revealed a statistically significant difference between the adjustment of ex-offenders who have utilized halfway house services and those who have not. Although as noted above halfway houses are generally assigned the higher-risk client with a more extensive criminal record, less stable employment history, and fewer community ties, residents' scores on the adjustment measure are significantly more favorable than scores of the comparison group. From this analysis, it is reasonable to argue that halfway houses offer services to ex-offenders which have a positive effect on their reintegration into the community. It is also reasonable to argue (if not conclude) that halfway houses accomplish two overall objectives as developed in Chapter III: to facilitate reintegration and protect society.

Even more salient than the significant effects of halfway houses is the difference in results if the operational definition of effectiveness and outcome were traditional indicators and no corrections were made for differences between the experimental and comparison groups. Results and policy conclusions would be paradoxically reversed if the evaluative design and outcome measures were less rigorous. The following section illustrates the results of the same data if examined with a different research design.

Let us assume that a non-equivalent comparison group quasi-experimental design had been chosen. The experimental group includes the same 236 former halfway house residents and the comparison group the same sample of 404 parolees released from institutions and not recipients of any halfway house services. The evaluator assumes the two groups are similar (except for the halfway house experience), and there is no need to correct for differences between the groups. This is quite common in criminal justice evaluations, as comparison groups are often chosen without due consideration of selection criteria.

Having drawn an experimental and comparison group, the evaluator needs only to collect outcome data and compare results between groups. Let us assume further that the traditional outcome measure for correctional programs (recidivism) had been chosen for use in the evaluation. Recidivism would be herein operationally defined as being "reimprisoned for either commission of a new crime or violation of parole or probation."

Data in Table 10 represent recidivism rates of the two groups without correcting for group differences, and using the above dichotomous definition of recidivism. Data would indicate that a

TABLE 10

RECIDIVISM RATES FOR HALFWAY HOUSE AND COMPARISON GROUPS

Group	N	Recidivism Rate	
Halfway house	215	13.5%	.001
Comparison	404	5.0%	

significantly greater proportion of the halfway house group than the comparison group are recidivists. These results contradict the earlier statement that halfway houses are more effectige than traditional aftercare modalities. In fact, an evaluator examining only these results would conclude that offenders do better when not sent to halfway houses and supervised only through parole and probation services.

The fastidious evaluator would further examine recidivism to determine reasons for offender reimprisonment. Table 11 illustrates a further analysis of the data in Table 10 .

TABLE 11

BEHAVIOR LEADING TO RECIDIVISM

	Group		
Level of Recidivism	Halfway House (N=215)	Comparison (N=404)	
Reimprisoned	13.5%(19)	5.0%(20)	.001
Reimprisoned for a new felony	5.6 (12)	4.2 (17)	.441
Reimprisoned for misdemeanor or technical violation	7.9 (17)	0.8 (3)	.001
Committed new felony, misdemeanor, or technical violation	50.2(108)	44.8(181)	.197
Committed new felony or misdemeanor	26.0 (56)	35.0(153)	.003

Although significantly more halfway house clients were reimprisoned than the comparison group of parolees, there was not a significant difference between those reimprisoned for a new felony offense. Suprisingly, differences in the rates result from the fact that a significantly greater proportion of halfway house clients were reimprisoned for misdemeanors or technical violations of parole or probation.

When the two populations are examined to determine the percentages committing a new offense or being charged with a technical violation, the halfway house group is found to have a greater percentage of clients in this category (although the difference is not significant). However, in contrast to the comparison group, the halfway house group has a significantly lower proportion of clients who committed a new misdemeanor or felony offense. The decision to re-process subjects through the criminal justice system is discretionary, and may not necessarily be a reflection of criminal behavior.

In summary, although the halfway house group had a significantly greater proportion of clients reimprisoned, a significantly lesser proportion of these clients committed new crimes. This is confusing, and could lead to inconclusive results. Any attempt to further explain the differences without knowing the characteristics of the two groups would be mere conjecture.

It should be obvious that using a dichotomous measure of outcome without correcting for differences in the groups can make a significant difference in the results of an evaluation. When the relative adjustment criterion was utilized (to include combined scales of criminal and acceptable behavior and correcting for group differences), halfway houses are found to yield significantly more favorable results than traditional aftercare supervision. However, without correcting for the selection processes, one would otherwise conclude that halfway house residents had significantly less favorable outcomes.

The difference in results is in part due to two processes: the use of disposition as a definition of recidivism, and the use of a dichotomous measure of recidivism. Using the disposition of the offense would penalize those persons having a more extensive prior offense record, making them appear to be poorer risks for remaining in the community. These high-risk offenders therefore receive a more severe disposition for the same offense than would someone with no prior record.

The dichotomous measure forces the evaluator to label several offenders as recidivists simply because they have committed minor crimes. However, when a graduated scale is utilized, ex-offenders would not need to be categorized as either failures or successes, but would merely be assigned a score indicating their relative adjustment.

The example above further reinforces the importance of utilizing a continuous outcome measure and for correcting for differences between the experimental and comparison groups. These allow a more valid comparative analysis, since the prior record (influencing the disposition)can be corrected for or equalized. A non-dispositional score also contributes to elimination of bias against a group considered a "higher risk."

FOOTNOTES - CHAPTER IV

1. Dennis C. Sullivan, Larry J. Seigel, and Todd Clear, "The Halfway House, Ten Years Later: Reappraisal of Correctional Innovation," Canadian Journal of Criminology and Corrections 16 (April 1974): 189.

2. Thorsten Sellin and Marvin E. Volfgang, Measurement of Delinquency (New York: John Wiley and Sons, 1964).

3. Marguerite Q. Warren, et al., Community Treatment Project: An Evaluation of Community Treatment for Delinquency, Fifth Progress Report (Sacramento: California Youth Authority and the National Institute of Mental Health, 1966), pp. 99-102.

4. Don M. Gottfredson and Kelly B. Ballard, The Validity of Two Parole Prediction Scales: An 8-Year Follow-up Study (Vacaville: California Department of Corrections, 1965), pp. 17-19.

5. Richard P. Seiter, A Statistical Model to Test the Effectiveness of the Ohio Halfway House Programs (Columbus: The Ohio State University Program for the Study of Crime and Delinquency, 1972), p. 18.

CHAPTER V

HALFWAY HOUSE EFFECTIVENESS
BY OFFENDER CATEGORY

The following analysis of halfway house resident outcome is designed to extend the measurement of outcome to provide halfway house administrators additional information concerning benefits received by clients. In categories the total halfway house group by selected background characteristics, it was possible to use analysis of covariance to measure the effectiveness of house services for each category of client. For example, by dividing house residents into four age categories and comparing outcome scores,[1] outcome results ("effectiveness") can be examined to identify age categories for which there is a significant difference between scores for the halfway house and comparison groups.

To determine the degree of benefit received by each resident category, comparisons were made between adjusted scores for the halfway house group and the comparison group. Adjusted scores provide a comparable measure, since original differences in group characteristics have been corrected by analysis of covariance. Therefore, the comparison group adjusted score is, in a sense, the expected score for the halfway house group had they not received house services. Differences between these two adjusted scores can reasonably be assumed to be an estimate of the benefit received from halfway house services. If differences in the halfway house adjusted scores exceed the comparison group adjusted score at the .05 level of significance, it can be argued that the resident group has received a significant benefit from the halfway house experience.

The second null hypothesis of Chapter I states that different classifications of halfway house residents cannot be differentiated in terms of outcome. The analysis below attempts to identify resident categories which receive significant benefit from house services, thereby providing a useful planning instrument to house administrators.

It is not the intent of this analysis to suggest that halfway houses should only provide services to a selected few. However, since almost all house residents are also under either parole or probation supervision, house administrators should be aware of the potential of their house to supplement parole or probation casework services for a variety of client categories. The cost for providing services is fairly consistent among categories of residents as they are divided in this analysis. It would therefore appear to be cost-effective to provide services to those selected residents to whom the house can provide maximum benefit. The analysis below also points out client categories for which there is no conclusive evidence of an effective level of benefit received. Knowledge of these deficiencies could, if house personnel so decide, result in possible program changes to increase house benefit to highlighted resident categories.

Data below illustrate the resident categories which have received a significant degree of benefit from house services. Although the degree of benefit received by some categories is not statistically significant, this does not necessarily lead to the conclusion that houses do not or cannot provide assistance to these residents. All that can be said is that no definitive conclusions can be made for these categories.

Relative Adjustment by Resident Characteristics

Data below include the "raw" and "adjusted" relative adjustment acores as well as levels of significance of differences between halfway house and comparison group adjusted scores within selected categories of the halfway house group. Resident characteristics have been examined individually, without development of complex interrelationships for combined characteristics and outcome. Since there are several criteria utilized in the resident selection process, analysis of characteristics singly limits the usefulness of the data in the decision-making process.

Resident status

Table 12 illustrates the outcome scores for parolees, probationers and federal pre-releasees. Data indicate that residents in halfway houses in the parolee and federal pre-releasee categories have a significantly more favorable relative adjustment than the comparison group;

TABLE 12

RELATIVE ADJUSTMENT BY RESIDENT STATUS

Resident Status	Half-way House Group N	Unadjusted Scores		Adjusted Scores		Level of Significance
		Half-way House	Comparison	Half-way House	Comparison	
Parolee	122	2.404	0.713	3.410	0.412	.04
Probationer	26	-0.838	0.713	1.729	0.548	.35
Federal	48	3.842	0.713	5.528	0.513	.01

both groups receiving a significant level of benefit from their stay at the houses. The effectiveness of houses in benefiting federal offenders suggests the need for a further examination of their status while in the house.

Federal offenders are assigned to halfway houses while serving the final months of their sentence before an expected parole date, and are required to reside at the house until that date. There are certain positive factors associated with the residential status of federal pre-releasees. House staff know the exact length of time the offender will be at the house, and can design a treatment program according to this time schedule. It also seems reasonable that offenders on pre-release status might approach their stay at the house with a more positive attitude than other offenders. This is due to the fact that the alternative to house residency is institutionalization (houses are therefore an extension of freedom for the pre-releasee), while other offenders residing in houses as an alternative to regular parole or probation might well perceive the halfway house as an additional restriction to their freedom.

It is reasonable to argue that, particularly for this sample, serving a portion of the sentence in an institution and the remainder in a community center has been demonstrated to be an effective correctional modality. The Ohio Department of Rehabilitation and Correction, within its program-priorities and long-range planning, might wish to consider the implementation of a pre-release program to allow inmates to reside in community centers prior to their parole release date and to take advantage of the positive factors inherent in a community-based program.

Race

Although there was very little difference between the relative outcome of Black and White halfway house clients (see Table 13), only the level of benefits (relative adjustment scores) received by Whites is statistically significant. The similar scores between Blacks and Whites suggest there may well be no difference between the ability of halfway houses to assist both Black and White clients, and houses should continue to service both groups according to their need for services.

TABLE 13

RELATIVE ADJUSTMENT BY RACE OF RESIDENT

Race of Resident	Half-way House Group N	Unadjusted Scores		Adjusted Scores		Level of Signi-ficance
		Half-way House	Compari-son	Half-way House	Compari-son	
White	212	2.393	0.713	3.581	0.360	.04
Black	75	2.217	0.713	3.491	0.477	.13

Educational Level

Some interesting results appear in Table 14. The level of

resident benefit is significant for those residents who have at least graduated from high school, and approximates the accepted level of significance for those with under an eighth grade education. It seems reasonable, since education is strongly related to occupational career, that there would be a gradient of increasing benefit as the level of education increases. However, data indicate that houses also provide a valuable benefit to residents with a lower level of education. This may be due to the fact that the needs of the lower educated group for educational, vocational, and other services are substantially addressed by the halfway house experience, and therefore this group receives a high level of benefit. Stated in a slightly different fashion, educational level may indicate different types and levels of needs by halfway house residents.

TABLE 14

RELATIVE ADJUSTMENT BY EDUCATIONAL LEVEL

Educational Level	Half-way House Group N	Unadjusted Scores		Adjusted Scores		Level of Significance
		Half-way House	Compari-son	Half-way House	Compari-son	
8 grades or less	77	2.188	0.713	3.386	0.488	.14
9 - 11 grades	89	1.511	0.713	3.004	0.388	.40
12 grades or more	39	3.862	0.713	4.894	0.614	.02

Age

Data in Table 15 also reflect some interesting results. In each age category, halfway house clients have higher scores than the comparison group, and the measure of benefit received is significant for clients over age 45. It is generally assumed that crime rates tend to decrease from the age of maximum criminality (adolescence) to the end of life, in part due to the "burn-out phenomenon."[2] Therefore, it might seem reasonable that aging of older clients reduce their criminal activity levels, and the potential for benefiting older residents in halfway houses in not significant.

This might well be true when considering only the reduction of criminal behavior among older clients. However, these residents require more assistance than younger residents in acceptable behavior criteria such as employment. Data indicate houses may well be most effective in assisting the older offender to raise his acceptable behavior scores by providing vocational and employment services. Although halfway houses might not have a significant effect on the reduction of criminal behavior among older offenders, houses appear to provide a valuable service in assisting these residents in their overall reintegration, as measured by both positive and negative behavior in the relative adjustment criterion.

TABLE 15

RELATIVE ADJUSTMENT BY AGE OF RESIDENT

Age of Resident	Half-way House Group N	Unadjusted Scores		Adjusted Scores		Level of Signi-ficance
		Half-way House	Compari-son	Half-way House	Compari-son	
25 years or less	72	2.075	0.713	4.101	0.352	.18
26 - 35 years	61	1.975	0.713	3.473	0.487	.25
36 - 45 years	41	2.327	0.713	2.578	0.688	.22
46 years or more	21	4.200	0.713	4.980	0.673	.05

Offense record

Data in Table 16 suggest that halfway houses are effective in providing a benefit to offenders with one or two prior felony offenses, and approximates a statistically significant benefit level to residents with from three to five prior felonies. Since sample sizes are small and variances large for those clients with either no or more than six prior offenses (affecting the level of significance), no valid conclusion can be drawn for these two categories; the results may be occurring by chance alone. However,

the difference in adjusted scores for halfway house and comparison
groups with more than six prior felony offenses is small, indicating the benefit received by those house residents is minimal.
House administrators might be assured of house effectiveness in
their efforts toward servicing middle-range offense clients, but
cannot be sure they are equipped to effectively assist clients
with several more prior felony offenses.

TABLE 16

RELATIVE ADJUSTMENT BY NUMBER OF PRIOR FELONY OFFENSES

Number of Prior Felony Offenses	Half-way House Group N	Unadjusted Scores		Adjusted Scores		Level of Signi-ficance
		Half-way House	Compari-son	Half-way House	Compari-son	
No prior felonies	7	2.857	0.713	5.163	0.673	.50
1 - 2 felonies	112	2.297	0.713	3.707	0.323	.05
3 - 5 felonies	60	2.517	0.713	3.943	0.502	.10
6 or more felonies	16	1.575	0.713	1.733	0.707	.68

When outcome scores by type of the offense (personal, property,
or victimless crime)[3] are examined in Table 17, data indicate that
houses provide some benefit to all residents, and a significant
level of benefit to perpetrators of crimes against the person.
Offenders who perpetrate crimes against the person, in contrast to
subjects in the comparison group, do significantly better (p .01)
in terms of relative adjustment. Those offenders who have committed victimless crimes (although small in number in this study)
have outcome scores that are close to being significantly different from the comparison group subjects. Those halfway house
clients who have perpetrated crimes against property, like their
comparison group counterparts, have the lowest scores of any of
these three offender types.

81

TABLE 17

RELATIVE ADJUSTMENT BY TYPE OF OFFENSE

Type of Offense	Half-way House Group N	Unadjusted Scores		Adjusted Scores		Level of Significan
		Half-way House	Comparison	Half-way House	Comparison	
Personal	27	4.933	0.713	5.808	0.655	.01
Property	152	1.680	0.713	2.811	0.288	.19
Victimless	16	4.056	0.713	6.979	0.598	.11

Prior incarcertaions

Data in the next two tables suggest benefit to resident categories by the length of the immediate past incarceration (Table 18), and the percentage of life incarcerated (Table 19). Data in Table 18 indicate a significant difference in outcome for offenders serving from one to two years for their last offense, while data in Table 19 indicate house residents who have been incarcerated between 1 and 10 percent of their lives have significantly more favorable outcome scores than their counterparts in the comparison group.

TABLE 18

RELATIVE ADJUSTMENT BY LENGTH OF LAST INCARCERATION

Length of Last Incarceration	Half-way House Group N	Unadjusted Scores		Adjusted Scores		Level of Significance
		Half-way House	Comparison	Half-way House	Comparison	
Less than 1 year	17	0.929	0.713	3.610	0.601	.92
1 - 2 years	122	2.340	0.713	3.556	0.349	.04
3 - 4 years	37	3.095	0.713	4.103	0.621	.09
5 years or more	20	2.005	0.713	3.118	0.658	.49

TABLE 19

RELATIVE ADJUSTMENT BY PERCENTAGE OF LIFE INCARCERATED

Percentage of Life Incarcerated	Half-way House Group N	Unadjusted Scores		Adjusted Scores		Level of Signi-ficance
		Half-way House	Compari-son	Half-way House	Compari-son	
Less than 1 percent	15	-0.647	0.713	2.502	0.596	.53
1 - 10 percent	48	3.008	0.713	4.416	0.546	.05
11 - 25 percent	72	2.319	0.713	3.843	0.460	.10
26 - 50 percent	55	1.498	0.713	3.168	0.486	.50
51 percent or more	9	-0.644	0.713	1.397	0.668	.63

This consistency of findings suggests it is reasonable to argue that houses are effective (as a transitional situation from the institution to the community) in providing services to offenders who have served a relatively short sentence and have not been incarcerated a large percentage of their lives. Outcome data are less encouraging for offenders who have served sentences of more than five years or have been incarcerated more than 25 percent of their lives.

Work history

Table 20 provides information regarding the relative adjustment of clients according to the percentage of their non-incarcerated lives for which they were employed. Data indicate that residents who had been employed 26 to 50 percent of their lives had significantly more favorable outcomes than the comparison group. This is perhaps due to the fact that these persons have developed work patterns beneficial to returning to society and the work routine.

It is also possible that residents who had worked only a small percentage of their lives had not been conditioned to a work routine, and initially require very basic counseling and vocational assistance before they could successfully be placed in jobs. Halfway houses provide support to residents who cannot immediately obtain jobs and support themselves, therefore allowing the resident an opportunity to improve his work skills, which in the long run could have a more positive effect in the reintegration process.

TABLE 20

RELATIVE ADJUSTMENT BY PERCENTAGE OF LIFE EMPLOYED

		Unadjusted Scores		Adjusted Scores		
Percentage of Life Employed	Half-way House Group N	Half-way House	Compari-son	Half-way House	Compari-son	Level of Signi-ficance
Less than 1 percent	28	2.489	0.713	5.374	0.513	.27
1 - 10 percent	70	1.960	0.713	3.697	0.412	.23
11 - 25 percent	50	1.318	0.713	2.647	0.549	.62
26 - 50 percent	39	3.538	0.713	4.040	0.665	.04
51 percent or more	8	5.338	0.713	4.129	0.737	.11

Previous drug and alcohol use

Each client's records were examined to determine if there was excessive use of drugs or alcohol. An excessive level was defined as staff's notation of use by a client which led to a problem the offender could not control or to his committing criminal offenses. Examination of resident drug and alsohol use indicates that clients without these problems score significantly higher in relative adjustment, indicating houses are effective in their services to these offenders. However, there is no conclusive evidence that houses are effective with clients who have major drug and alcohol problems (see Table 21).

Most halfway houses are designed to provide services to a broad typology of residents, without emphasizing treatment for any one resident category. Perhaps a more structured and single-objective program may be most effective with offenders with major alcohol or drug problems. For example, Fresh Start, catering exclusively to the alcoholic offender, has shown relatively good success with a specialized treatment program for the alcoholic

offender. The program at Fresh Start initially focuses on the
alcohol problem of clients; only after the resident has "dried out"
and realizes his problem do Fresh Start staff begin reintegrative
services such as emphasizing beginning employment.

TABLE 21

RELATIVE ADJUSTMENT BY PREVIOUS ALCOHOL AND DRUG USE

Alcohol or Drug Use	Half-way House Group N	Unadjusted Scores		Adjusted Scores		Level of Significance
		Half-way House	Compari-son	Half-way House	Compari-son	
Alcohol						
Excessive use	64	1.163	0.713	2.865	0.444	.68
No excessive use	131	2.894	0.713	3.789	0.423	.01
Drug						
Excessive use	45	1.276	0.713	5.197	0.277	.66
No excessive use	150	2.641	0.713	3.265	0.481	.01

Summary

Outcomes in this chapter of the study can be interpreted to
suggest some guidelines as to the types of clients with whom halfway house programs have been effective. By using analysis of
covariance and comparing adjusted scores of the halfway house and
comparison groups, a measure of "benefit" received from houses
has been developed. This measure of benefit is preferred to a
simple comparison of unadjusted outcome scores between residents.
This latter measure would provide indicators of the outcome for
resident categories, but would not suggest whether the outcome was
due to the halfway house experience or would have occurred within
regular methods of correctional treatment.

Data in the above section reveal interesting findings about
categories of residents who receive a significant level of benefit
from house services. Results do not always correspond to what

might be pre-conceived hypotheses. Therefore, these findings are valuable to the correctional administrator who attempts to pre-scribe programs for various categories of clients, yet must act on intuition, without knowledge of the ability of certain programs to assist certain clients.

Halfway houses have been shown to provide a significant level of benefit to a wide variety of residents, even though attempts to cater to all categories of clients may reduce house effectiveness. It has been pointed out that "more must be learned about the types of offenders who can best benefit from the various types of (halfway house) programs, and about the kinds of residential popu-lation balances best designed to produce optimum results."[4] House administrators should make use of the information provided, either for selection of residents or development of additional programs for resident categories for which there is to date no conclusive evidence of received benefit.

FOOTNOTES - CHAPTER V

1. Outcome scores for this analysis were the adjusted raw scores, after correction for differences between the comparison and halfway house groups. Scores have been "adjusted" to reflect equalization of groups by the use of analysis of covariance.

2. Walter C. Reckless, The Crime Problem, 5th Ed. (New York: Appleton-Century-Crofts, 1973), p. 81; Edwin H. Sutherland and Donald R. Cressey, Criminology, 8th Ed. (Philadelphia: J.B. Lippincott Company, 1970), p. 124.

3. The categories of crimes included in each classification are:

Personal	Property	Victimless
Murder	Burglary	Drug offenses
Manslaughter	Malicious destruction	Homosexuality
All assaults	of property	Prostitution
Rape/sex offenses	All larceny	Gambling
	Auto theft	
	Robbery	

4. Center for Studies of Crime and Delinquency, Graduated Release (Washington, D.C.: National Institute of Mental Health, 1971), p. 21.

CHAPTER VI

PROJECTING FUTURE LOADS AND COSTS FOR PROGRAMS

As was noted in Chapter II, an important element of an evaluation is the accumulation and presentation of data to assist the administrator in the planning process. Although many such evaluations conclude with recommendations based on analysis of effectiveness, the development of projections reflecting program loads might be extremely beneficial to users of the evaluation.

The third null hypothesis as stated in Chapter I is that changes in policy will have no effect on the future loads of halfway houses or costs to the correctional system. This chapter presents resulting house loads and system costs if various policies were implemented, thereby testing whether changes in correctional policy would, in fact, have significant implications for halfway house planning.

This chapter illustrates the use of a mathematical model to project loads for Ohio halfway houses over a ten-year period. To determine loads, halfway houses are examined as "states" within the overall correctional system. Costs for each state have been added to the model, allowing projections of costs for the system over the same period.

To add flexibility to projections, possible policy changes that could occur over the ten-year period were simulated and the probable impact of such changes on the loads and costs of the several states in the system examined. Thus the model serves as an experimental resource for planning purposes.

Markov Processes

One mathematical model useful for projecting system loads and costs, and basic in its approach and operations, is a Markov process. The Markov process can be characterized by the following:

    1. The system is described as a set of "states." These

states are interpreted herein as a location of an individual in the process, described according to the principal characteristics studied. For instance one could describe a person being in a state labeled ("Ohio prison," or "regular parole supervision," or any one of the halfway houses).

2. There exist chances for a person to go from one state to another. These "transitions" are described in probabilistic terms. The transition probabilities are obtained from the empirical information collected during the study (--average length of stay in each state, and loads going from one state to another).

3. The transitions that are allowed are treated as a function of time. In this model the probabilities are defined as "the probability of going from one state to another in one (month)."

4. The transition probabilities are also a function of which state of being the individual is in. Hence, where the individual is (next month) depends on where he is (this month) and is in no way a function of where he was prior to (this month). This can be a severe limitation on the applicability of the Markov model in some situations.

5. By considering a large number of people in the process . . . the model will yield the average number of people in each state, such as ("the average number of residents in each halfway house per month," or "the number of persons under parole supervision each month.")

6. Finally, by superimposing costs on a per case per (month) basis, over the expected loads in each state, one can utilize the model structure as an accounting aid in determining expected system costs.[1]

The primary information needed to support the development of a Markov model are measurements or estimates of the transition probabilities, the total population in the system (or, if available, estimates of average loads for the states), and the costs associated with state occupancy. Frequently, in developing this sort of model, one discovers that key data elements are not available. The data must then be estimated on the basis of the best available information and, if the model is to be used as a device for a planning or management decisions, the sensitivity of the output to the estimates determined.

For this particular model, data were collected from all Ohio adult halfway houses to determine house loads, costs, and transition probabilities. The Ohio Department of Rehabilitation and Correction provided information on institutional, parole, and furlough loads and costs, while the United States Bureau of Prisons provided the same information for Ohio offenders under federal supervision.[2]

Present System Model

Presented next is a descriptive model of the present correctional system, including the loads and costs of each state, and the transitional probabilities of moving from one state to another. The present system was constructed from the analysis of data for 1973. Since that time, certain changes in programs have been made that are reflected in the following section on predicted changes.

Markov model state descriptions

The present system includes eighteen states, beginning with the incarcerated offender, moving through parole or halfway house supervision, and ending with either a recidivism state or the "free" state of being released from supervision. Following the definitions of states in Table 22, the system flow chart of Figure 3 illustrates the possible transitions through the states as assumed in the model.

From Ohio prisons, offenders can go to parole, furlough, or free states, but all federal prisoners go directly to regular supervision or a community facility. From parole, offenders can go to regular supervision, one of the ten halfway houses, or another facility. Furloughees initially go to a halfway house or another facility. All free state persons return to a federal or state prison at the same percentage as they had exited. Subjects on regular supervision can stay in that state, go to the free state, or recidivate (law/court). Halfway house residents go either to regular supervision, the free state, the recidivism state, or stay at the house. Residents at other facilities all go to the free state, and recidivists flow into either Ohio or federal prisons.

TABLE 22

MARKOV MODEL STATE DESCRIPTIONS

1. Federal Prison. This includes all Ohio residents in federal prisons who will be returning to Ohio on parole, placed in a community correctional center, or released without further supervision.

2. Ohio Prison. This state includes offenders incarcerated in any of Ohio's seven institutions or in the medical center. This state supplies the largest number of offenders which will be processed through the system.

3. Parole. This state includes all incarcerated offenders who leave an Ohio or federal institution by way of parole, shock parole, shock probation, furlough, or transfer to a community correctional center. This is only a status or dummy state, and no cost is involved.

4. Furlough. All incarcerated offenders having state institutions on a work or educational furlough status are included in this state. It, too, is merely a status state, and no cost is involved.

5. Free. This state serves a dual purpose. It includes those offenders released after maximum expiration of their sentence who have no parole supervision and therefore no cost. It also acts as a feedback and stabilizing state for those being released from parole supervision. The model is stabilized as all these people are fed back into a prison system so the model does not exhaust itself.

6. Regular Parole Supervision. All offenders from the parole state under regular supervision, rather than in a halfway house, are included in this state.

7-16. Halfway Houses. Each halfway house involved in the study has been analyzed separately. This is imperative since each house has different space limits and accepts residents from other states differentially.

17. Other Facility. This state includes those offenders who are placed in a community facility other than a halfway house. Both federal and Ohio correctional departments contract with agencies such as Volunteers of America, Salvation Army, and YMCA.

18. Law/Court. This is the recidivism state for those offenders who commit a new crime and are returned to the institution. Unlike the feedback from the "Free" state (Number 5), there is a cost assigned for the processing of these recidivists through the criminal justice system.

Transition probabilities

The eighteen states of the model interact with each other through the flow of people from one state to another. The most straightforward mathematical representation of the state-space description of the system utilizes matrices. By arranging the states as the identifiers for the rows and columns of a square matrix, it is possible to represent every possible interaction among the states in terms of the transition probabilities. By multiplying a vector indicating the number of people (the load) in each state by the square matrix of transition probabilities, one obtains a new vector indicating the expected number of people in each state after one transition (after one month for the model formulation used herein). By continuing this multiplication process, one is able to simulate the activities of the system represented by the Markov model for any desired period of time.

Table 23 presents the transition probabilities for the model. The information upon which the transition probabilities are based came directly from empirical data of external movements through the system. Computation of the probabilities included calculating the proportion of the population in each state going to each of the other allowed states, determining the average length of stay in each state, and pro-rating the state output accordingly.

The initial loads of the model are also included in Table 23. These are the average monthly loads for each state over 1973, as computed from data gathered from the agencies.

Present system costs

One of the desired characteristics of such a model is an ability to facilitate cost analysis of alternative system programs. The Markov model developed has this desirable characteristic in that it provides a simple straightforward framework for summing costs, based on the dollar amount per case per month for that state. Costs are only the costs to the correctional system, and do not represent costs incurred when offenders receive services from some other social welfare agencies.

92

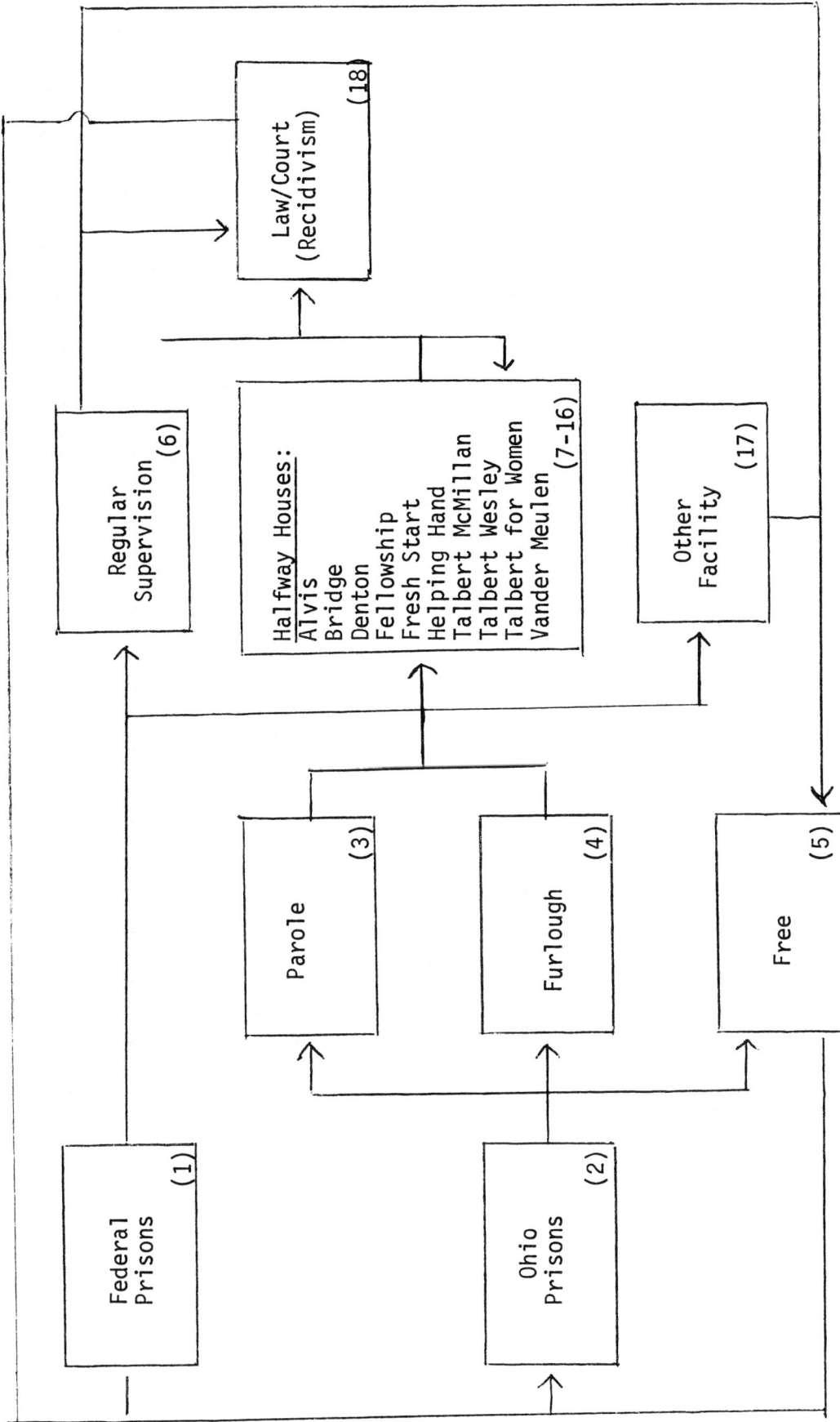

FIGURE 3: POSSIBLE TRANSITION THROUGH THE CORRECTIONAL SYSTEM

TABLE 23

TRANSITION PROBABILITIES AND COSTS FOR CORRECTIONAL SYSTEM STATES

STATES	Initial Load	Monthly Cost Per Case	(1) Federal Prison	(2) Ohio Prison	(3) Parole	(4) Furlough	(5) Free	(6) Regular Supervision	(7) Alvis House	(8) Bridge House	(9) Denton House	(10) Fellowship House	(11) Fresh Start	(12) Helping Hand	(13) Talbert McMillan	(14) Talbert Wesley	(15) Talbert for Women	(16) Vander Meulen	(17) Other Facility	(18) Law/Court
(1) Federal Prison	784	446.7	.9560					.0213	.0035	.0001	.0025	.0000	.0000	.0086	.0039	.0039	.0002	.0000	.0000	.0000
(2) Ohio Prison	7879	391.8		.9538	.0437	.0025														
(3) Parole	344.6	0.0						.823	.016	.009	.014	.004	.009	.016	.007	.005	.006	.012	.079	.003
(4) Furlough	19.75	0.0							.260	.043	.105	.022	.010	.150	.054	.054	.007	.090	.205	.004
(5) Free	150	0.0	.090	.910																
(6) Regular Supervision	4135	38.70					.066	.857												.077
(7) Alvis House	54	356.7						.189	.800										.008	.003
(8) Bridge House	18	412.5						.210		.765									.019	.006
(9) Denton House	50	450.0						.129			.863								.004	.004
(10) Fellowship House	11	301.5						.168				.804							.012	.016
(11) Fresh Start	13	300.0						.148					.845						.007	.000
(12) Helping Hand	72	322.8						.173						.815					.007	.005
(13) Talbert McMillan	16	508.5						.257							.722				.000	.021
(14) Talbert Wesley	15	488.4						.159								.800			.019	.022
(15) Talbert for Women	15	549.9						.139									.854		.000	.007
(16) Vander Meulen	10	300.0						.398										.559	.033	.010
(17) Other Facility	25	325.8					1.000													
(18) Law/Court	23.78	550.0	.090	.910																

94

Although reliable information was available in developing costs of various states, cost figures do not represent a cost-benefit analysis or measure of economic efficiency. The cost data are intended to provide reasonable indications of the economic sensitivity of the system to hypothesized programs. The emphasis is on the use of dollars or dollar equivalents as a meaningful measure of total system impact of potential programs.

The monthly costs for each state are presented in the transition matrix of Table 23. Monthly costs for federal and state institutions were, once again, obtained from the Ohio Department of Rehabilitation and Correction and the United States Bureau of Prisons. They represent variable costs, excluding any facility costs. Parole and furlough are transitional status states and reflect no cost figure. The free state is a no cost figure, since the offender is not supervised in that state.

Regular supervision is a combination of the costs of supervising both federal and Ohio parolees, weighted according to the loads of each type of caseload. Ohio costs for parole supervision in 1973 were $392 per year and federal costs were $1,200 per year. Halfway house costs are computed monthly variable costs for providing residence and services to clients. These are total house variable costs, rather than the partial subsidy payments made by Ohio and federal correctional systems in contracting for house services. The cost of other facilities is an estimate, based in part on knowledge of their costs and in part on knowledge of what correctional agencies pay to contract for services.

The law/court state is an estimated calculation of the cost to police, prosecutors, and courts in arresting, processing and convicting offenders. Estimates were made after conversations with officials throughout the criminal justice system. Again, there are some limits of the cost analysis due to the estimates of some states.

Monthly state costs have been multiplied by the monthly loads to obtain system costs at the end of each twelve month period. Data in Table 24 represent the total costs to the correctional system for operation in the stable or present states, projected

95

annually for the next ten years. If present policies were to continue and loads remain stable, the variable system costs over the next ten years have been calculated to be $42,700,660.

TABLE 24

ANNUAL VARIABLE SYSTEM COST

Year	Annual Cost	Accumulated Cost
1	$4,270,090	$4,270,090
2	4,270,040	8,540,130
3	4,270,050	12,810,180
4	4,270,060	17,080,240
5	4,270,070	21,350,310
6	4,270,070	35,620,380
7	4,270,070	29,890,450
8	4,270,070	34,160,520
9	4,270,070	38,430,590
10	4,270,070	42,700,660

Present system loads

Initial loads were determined by computing the average monthly population in each state from data provided by the agencies involved. Due to the problem of entering a mobile system with a static model, loads need to be adjusted or stabilized, accomplished by letting the Markov process compute loads with no policy changes over a ten-year period. Stabilized loads of the actual correctional population are more realistic and can be used as bases for hypothesized changes in policies. Table 25 illustrates beginning and stable loads. The following sections of this chapter illustrate the effect on system loads and costs if several optional policies were implemented. Results indicate system loads and costs if some policy changes were made separately, or others made simultaneously.

Option 1: Shock parole using halfway houses

This option hypothesized that Ohio's recent shock parole statute would increase the number of men paroled from Ohio institutions by 50 parolees per month. Furthermore, it was hypothesized

TABLE 25

BEGINNING AND STABILIZED MONTHLY SYSTEM LOADS

State	Beginning Monthly Load	Stabilized Monthly Load
(1) Federal Prison	784.0	918.0
(2) Ohio Prison	7879.0	8836.0
(3) Parole	344.6	386.0
(4) Furlough	19.8	22.2
(5) Free	220.0	226.6
(6) Regular Supervision	4135.0	2851.0
(7) Alvis	54.0	75.0
(8) Bridge	18.0	19.3
(9) Denton	50.0	72.9
(10) Fellowship	11.0	10.4
(11) Fresh Start	13.0	23.9
(12) Helping Hand	72.0	94.1
(13) Talbert McMillan	16.0	27.0
(14) Talbert Wesley	15.0	33.7
(15) Talbert for Women	15.0	18.3
(16) Vander Meulen	10.0	15.0
(17) Other Facility	25.0	38.4
(18) Law/Court	210.0	222.4

that the added parolees would be distributed to regular supervision and community correctional centers with the same
transitional probabilities as regular parolees. Table 26 illustrates the new state loads resulting from the option

The load data on this option indicate that there is not a
significant increase in halfway house residents resulting from
this policy. Although each house would gain a few residents, the
major changes are a reduction in Ohio prisons and an increase
under regular parole supervision. However, even these changes
are relatively small. By only releasing 50 inmates per month or
600 per year, there is a rather minute change on the loads of

the system.

As indicated in Table 27, there is a corresponding reduction in the system cost when operationalizing this option. By implementing this option, the annual cost is consistently reduced by 2.1 percent over each yearly period for the next ten years. However, larger increases in the number of inmates released on shock parole would result in larger corresponding savings in institutional variable costs.

TABLE 26

OPTION 1:   SHOCK PAROLE USING HALFWAY HOUSES

State	Present Load	Load after Year				
		1	2	3	5	10
1	918.0	933.8	955.6	969.0	981.3	987.0
2	8836.0	8533.1	8492.3	8478.0	8465.6	8459.9
3	386.0	422.2	419.9	419.1	418.5	418.2
4	22.2	21.4	21.3	21.3	21.2	21.2
5	226.6	242.4	243.6	243.6	243.5	243.5
6	2851.0	3051.8	3069.4	3070.0	3069.6	3069.4
7	75.0	78.1	78.0	78.2	78.3	78.4
8	19.3	20.6	20.5	20.4	20.4	20.4
9	72.9	75.9	76.2	76.4	76.6	76.7
10	10.4	11.0	11.0	11.0	10.9	10.9
11	23.9	25.8	25.8	25.7	25.7	25.7
12	94.1	97.1	97.8	98.4	99.0	99.3
13	27.0	28.0	28.2	28.4	28.6	28.6
14	33.7	34.6	34.9	35.2	35.4	35.4
15	18.3	19.6	19.7	19.6	19.6	19.6
16	15.0	15.9	15.8	15.8	15.7	15.7
17	38.4	41.3	41.0	41.0	40.9	40.9
18	222.4	237.6	239.3	239.4	239.4	239.4

Option 2: Shock parolees go to regular supervision

It is possible that residents receiving shock parole would be low risk cases with substantial community ties and would not need halfway house services. Although it is more likely that the number of shock parolees assigned to halfway houses will vary somewhere

98

TABLE 27

ACCUMULATED TEN YEAR SYSTEM COST FOR OPTION 1

Year	Present Policy	Option Policy	% Difference
1	$ 4,270,090	$ 4,182,210	-2.1%
2	8,540,130	8,360,210	-2.1
3	12,810,180	12,539,120	-2.1
4	17,080,240	16,518,740	-2.1
5	21,350,310	20,898,780	-2.1
6	25,620,380	25,079,060	-2.1
7	29,890,450	29,259,480	-2.1
8	34,160,520	33,439,480	-2.1
9	38,430,590	37,620,550	-2.1
10	42,700,660	41,801,150	-2.1

between Option 1 and this latter option, this option examines the hypothesis that no shock parolees will be assigned to halfway houses.

Table 28 illustrates that this option would have no appreciable effect on halfway house loads, since the resulting decrease in the institutional population would only increase the regular supervision state. Table 29 illustrates the savings which would correspond to a change in policy to Option 2. There is very little difference in the cost of Option 1 and Option 2; Option 2 reduced the present policy cost by 2 percent over the next ten years.

Option 3: Furlough 30 inmates per month

This option would test the effect of increasing the number of institutionalized offenders released under the Ohio furlough program. Initial objectives of the furlough program were to release 30 inmates per month, but as of yet this goal has not been reached. It is therefore a realistic hypothesis to test the effect of this increase. Furloughees will be placed, in this option, in various halfway houses at the same proportions as they were actually assigned.

Data in Table 30 illustrate how the increase would be distributed among the halfway houses. The resident populations of all houses would be increased to accomodate the expanded furlough program. As seen in Table 31, there is very little difference in the system cost when the furlough program is increased to release 30 inmates per month.

TABLE 28

OPTION 2: SHOCK PAROLEES GO TO REGULAR SUPERVISION

State	Present Load	Load after Year				
		1	2	3	5	10
1	918.0	936.3	958.6	972.2	984.6	990.4
2	8836.0	8856.8	8520.9	8507.1	8494.6	8488.8
3	386.0	374.5	372.7	372.1	371.7	371.2
4	22.2	21.5	21.4	21.4	21.3	21.3
5	226.6	241.4	242.4	242.3	242.3	242.2
6	2851.0	3096.2	3109.9	3109.9	3109.6	3109.3
7	75.0	74.6	74.4	74.5	74.7	74.8
8	19.3	18.8	18.7	18.6	18.6	18.6
9	72.9	72.0	71.6	71.7	71.0	72.0
10	10.4	10.1	10.0	10.0	10.0	10.0
11	23.9	23.4	23.1	23.0	23.0	22.9
12	94.1	93.4	93.9	94.5	95.2	95.5
13	27.0	26.8	27.1	27.3	27.4	27.5
14	33.7	33.5	33.8	34.1	34.4	34.5
15	18.3	18.0	17.8	17.7	17.7	17.7
16	15.0	14.6	14.5	14.5	14.5	14.4
17	38.4	37.3	37.1	37.1	37.0	37.0
18	222.4	240.9	242.3	242.3	242.3	242.3

TABLE 29

ACCUMULATED TEN YEAR SYSTEM COST FOR OPTION 2

Year	Present Policy	Option Policy	% Difference
1	$ 4,270,090	$ 4,186,550	-2.0%
2	8,540,130	8,370,100	-2.0
3	12,810,180	12,554,700	-2.0
4	17,080,240	16,740,020	-2.0
5	21,350,310	20,925,760	-2.0
6	25,620,380	25,111,740	-2.0
7	29,890,450	29,297,860	-2.0
8	34,160,520	33,484,070	-2.0
9	38,430,590	37,670,340	-2.0
10	42,700,660	41,856,640	-2.0

TABLE 30

OPTION 3: FURLOUGH 30 INMATES PER MONTH

State	Present Load	Load after Year				
		1	2	3	5	10
1	918.0	919.9	923.0	925.2	927.3	928.2
2	8836.0	8779.4	8767.5	8764.6	8762.1	8761.1
3	386.0	384.0	383.4	383.3	383.2	383.1
4	22.2	30.0	30.0	30.0	30.0	30.0
5	226.6	229.2	229.6	229.7	229.7	229.7
6	2851.0	2866.2	2872.2	2873.0	2873.0	2873.0
7	75.0	85.1	85.8	85.9	85.9	85.9
8	19.3	20.6	20.6	20.6	20.6	20.6
9	72.9	77.6	78.5	78.6	78.7	78.7
10	10.4	11.2	11.2	11.2	11.2	11.2
11	23.9	24.2	24.2	24.2	24.2	24.2
12	94.1	99.8	100.3	100.5	100.6	100.6
13	27.0	28.5	28.6	28.6	28.6	28.6
14	33.7	35.6	35.8	35.8	35.9	35.9
15	18.3	18.5	18.5	18.5	18.5	18.5
16	15.0	16.6	16.6	16.5	16.5	16.5
17	38.4	40.1	40.1	40.1	40.0	40.0
18	222.4	223.6	224.2	224.3	224.3	224.3

TABLE 31

ACCUMULATED TEN YEAR SYSTEM COST FOR OPTION 3

Year	Present Policy	Option Policy	% Difference
1	$ 4,270,090	$ 4,261,350	-0.2%
2	8,540,130	8,520,920	-0.2
3	12,810,180	12,780,430	-0.2
4	17,080,240	17,040,020	-0.2
5	21,350,310	21,299,670	-0.2
6	25,620,380	25,559,350	-0.2
7	29,890,450	29,819,050	-0.2
8	34,160,520	34,078,760	-0.2
9	38,430,590	38,338,480	-0.2
10	42,700,660	42,598,210	-0.2

Option 4: Furlough 50 inmates per month

It is possible that the furlough program would expand even beyond the initial objectives of Adult Parole Authority administrators. This option examines the effect of expanding the furlough release program to 50 inmates per month. If transition probabilities remain stable, Table 32 indicates that while all house populations would expand, Alvis, Denton, and Helping Hand would have the greatest increases. Table 33 indicates a very modest reduction in cost by adopting this option. It is reasonable to conclude that the furlough program can be expanded without increasing the total cost to the correctional system.

Option 5: Furlough program ended

It is also important to examine the effect on halfway houses if the furlough program were ended. During the latter part of 1974, due to financial restraints on the Ohio Department of Rehabilitation and Correction, very few furloughees were released. Table 34 illustrates the system effect of such a policy change. Those houses that accomodate a large percentage of furlough releasees would gain the most residents if the furlough program were expanded, and would also be hurt the most in numbers if the program were deleted. However, the loss of these residents to smaller houses such as Fellowship and Vander Meulen would be critical. These smaller houses, which rely on state furlough contracts for a large portion of their income, could conceivably be forced to close their facilities. Before a policy such as this option is undertaken, consideration should be given to the effect on the private facilities which would be affected.

No only would the discontinuance of the furlough program have a critical effect on halfway houses, but it would also result in a small increase in cost to the correctional system (Table 35).

Option 6: Increase regular parole and furlough

It is also possible to use the Markov model for simultaneously changing more than one policy. This option calculates the

TABLE 32

OPTION 4: FURLOUGH 50 INMATES PER MONTH

State	Present Load	Load after Year				
		1	2	3	5	10
1	918.0	924.7	935.4	942.7	949.7	953.0
2	8836.0	8641.7	8602.2	8591.9	8584.6	8581.3
3	386.0	378.2	376.2	375.7	375.4	375.3
4	22.2	49.2	49.0	49.0	48.9	48.9
5	226.6	236.7	237.1	237.2	237.2	237.2
6	2851.0	2404.6	2924.8	2927.0	2927.2	2927.1
7	75.0	108.0	110.3	110.3	110.3	110.3
8	19.3	23.8	23.8	23.8	23.8	23.8
9	72.9	89.4	92.2	92.7	92.8	92.9
10	10.4	13.1	13.2	13.2	13.2	13.1
11	23.9	25.1	25.0	25.0	25.0	24.9
12	94.1	113.7	115.6	116.0	116.3	116.5
13	27.0	32.1	32.2	32.3	32.4	32.5
14	33.7	40.4	40.9	41.1	41.2	41.3
15	18.3	19.2	19.2	19.2	19.1	19.1
16	15.0	20.4	20.3	20.2	20.2	20.2
17	38.4	44.2	44.1	44.0	44.0	44.0
18	222.4	226.8	228.7	228.9	229.0	229.0

TABLE 33

ACCUMULATED TEN YEAR SYSTEM COST FOR OPTION 4

Year	Present Policy	Option Policy	% Difference
1	$ 4,270,090	$ 4,239,820	-0.7%
2	8,540,130	8,473,770	-0.8
3	12,810,180	12,707,590	-0.8
4	17,080,240	16,941,720	-0.8
5	21,350,310	21,176,060	-0.8
6	25,620,380	25,410,530	-0.8
7	29,890,450	29,645,070	-0.8
8	34,160,520	33,879,650	-0.8
9	38,430,590	38,114,250	-0.8
10	42,700,660	42,348,870	-0.8

TABLE 34

OPTION 5: FURLOUGH PROGRAM ENDED

State	Present Load	Load after Year				
		1	2	3	5	10
1	918.0	912.7	904.0	897.8	892.0	889.2
2	8836.0	8991.0	9026.3	9035.8	9042.4	9045.6
3	386.0	393.0	394.7	395.1	395.4	395.6
4	22.2	0.0	0.0	0.0	0.0	0.0
5	226.6	219.2	217.9	217.8	217.8	217.8
6	2851.0	2807.3	2790.2	2787.9	2787.6	2787.5
7	75.0	49.8	47.6	47.4	47.3	47.3
8	19.3	15.6	15.5	15.5	15.6	15.6
9	72.9	59.6	57.0	56.6	56.4	56.3
10	10.4	8.2	8.1	8.1	8.1	8.1
11	23.9	22.9	22.9	22.9	23.0	23.0
12	94.1	78.3	76.5	76.1	75.8	75.6
13	27.0	27.4	22.8	22.7	22.6	22.6
14	33.7	28.3	27.7	27.6	27.4	27.4
15	18.3	17.5	17.5	17.6	17.5	17.5
16	15.0	10.7	10.7	10.7	10.8	10.8
17	38.4	33.7	33.8	33.8	33.8	33.8
18	222.4	218.8	217.2	217.0	216.9	216.9

TABLE 35

ACCUMULATED TEN YEAR SYSTEM COST FOR OPTION 5

Year	Present Policy	Option Policy	% Difference
1	$ 4,270,090	$ 4,294,580	+0.6
2	8,540,130	8,594,280	+0.6
3	12,810,180	12,894,260	+0.7
4	17,080,240	17,194,050	+0.7
5	21,350,310	21,493,700	+0.7
6	25,620,380	25,793,260	+0.7
7	29,890,450	30,092,760	+0.7
8	34,160,520	34,392,240	+0.7
9	38,430,590	38,691,710	+0.7
10	42,700,660	42,991,170	+0.7

effect of releasing an additional 100 inmates per month on regular parole and another 50 on furlough. This would not be an unreasonable policy if the Department of Rehabilitation and Correction adopted such a stance more committed both to the use of community corrections and reducing institutional populations.

Table 36 illustrates the ten-year load projections if this policy were implemented. Data indicate adoption of such a policy would reverse the present trend of an increasing Ohio institutional population (State 2), and increase the number under regular parole supervision (all of the increased parole releasees have been added directly to State 6). Halfway house populations would also be increased due to the increased use of furlough.

An examination of the projected costs (Table 37) indicates a savings of between 5 and 6 percent if this policy were adopted. Parole supervision is less costly than institutionalization, and results in savings in excess of $230,000 per year to the total correctional system. Although this is a mathematical model, it still points to some obvious advantages of the increased reliance on community-based rather than institutional corrections.

Option 7: Work release program

Ohio has constitutional restrictions against correctional inmates' working for or in competition with private businesses. If this law were repealed, a work release program could be developed in which institutional inmates were allowed to leave the institution to work during the day, returning to institutional supervision at night. As indicated in Table 38, if this option only included incarcerated inmates, there would be no effect on future loads of halfway houses. The only load changes would be between Ohio prisons and an added state (number 19) of work release. Option 7 would place 25 percent of the prison population in a work release program.

The major change in this program is the cost factor. If work release inmates were asked to pay for food and living accomodations, this would cut the cost to the system. A modest administrative cost of $5.00 per person per month has been assigned

TABLE 36

OPTION 6:   INCREASE REGULAR PAROLE BY 100 AND FURLOUGH BY 50

| State | Present Load | Load after Year | | | | |
		1	2	3	5	10
1	918.0	969.8	1034.7	1074.3	1109.9	1126.1
2	8836.0	7893.1	7771.1	7732.2	7699.8	7685.2
3	386.0	346.2	340.0	338.2	336.7	336.1
4	22.2	70.1	68.8	68.5	68.1	68.0
5	226.6	274.7	277.8	277.6	277.2	277.0
6	2851.0	3465.1	3513.7	3512.8	3509.2	3507.5
7	75.0	132.9	134.8	134.9	135.0	135.1
8	19.3	26.7	26.2	26.0	25.9	25.8
9	72.9	101.6	105.2	106.0	106.4	106.6
10	10.4	14.9	14.7	14.6	14.5	14.5
11	23.9	25.1	24.4	24.1	24.0	23.9
12	94.1	128.9	132.4	134.1	135.8	136.6
13	27.0	35.9	36.4	46.9	37.4	37.6
14	33.7	45.7	47.0	47.8	48.5	48.9
15	18.3	19.3	18.9	18.8	18.7	18.7
16	15.0	24.0	23.3	23.2	23.1	23.0
17	38.4	46.7	45.9	45.7	45.6	45.5
18	222.4	269.7	274.6	274.6	274.3	274.2

TABLE 37

ACCUMULATED TEN YEAR SYSTEM COST FOR OPTION 6

Year	Present Policy	Option Policy	% Difference
1	$ 4,270,090	$ 4,039,510	-5.4%
2	8,540,130	8,068,010	-5.5
3	12,810,180	12,100,080	-5.5
4	17,080,240	16,134,760	-5.5
5	21,350,310	20,170,960	-5.5
6	25,620,380	24,208,020	-5.5
7	29,890,450	28,245,570	-5.5
8	34,160,520	32,283,410	-5.5
9	38,430,590	36,321,420	-5.5
10	42,700,660	40,359,520	-5.5

TABLE 38

OPTION 7: WORK RELEASE PROGRAM

State	Present Load	Load after Year 1	2	3	5	10
1	918.0	917.0	915.7	914.9	914.1	913.7
2	8836.0	6594.2	6595.2	6595.1	6596.1	6595.1
3	386.0	384.3	384.4	384.5	384.5	384.5
4	22.2	22.1	22.1	22.1	22.1	22.1
5	226.6	225.6	225.5	225.5	225.5	225.5
6	2851.0	2837.5	2837.3	2837.2	2837.3	2837.3
7	75.0	75.5	75.5	75.5	75.5	75.5
8	19.3	19.2	19.2	19.2	19.2	19.2
9	72.9	72.6	72.6	72.6	72.6	72.5
10	10.4	10.3	10.3	10.3	10.3	10.3
11	23.9	23.8	23.7	23.7	23.7	23.8
12	94.1	93.8	93.8	93.7	93.7	93.7
13	27.0	27.0	26.9	26.9	26.9	26.9
14	33.7	33.6	33.6	33.6	33.5	33.5
15	18.3	18.2	18.2	18.2	18.2	18.2
16	15.0	15.0	15.0	15.0	15.0	15.0
17	38.4	38.2	38.2	38.2	38.2	38.2
18	222.4	221.4	221.3	221.3	221.3	221.3
19					2197.5	2197.9

TABLE 39

ACCUMULATED TEN YEAR SYSTEM COST FOR OPTION 7

Year	Present Policy	Option Policy	% Difference
1	$ 4,270,090	$ 3,400,940	-20.4%
2	8,540,130	6,801,530	-20.4
3	12,810,180	10,201,700	-20.4
4	17,080,240	13,601,640	-20.4
5	21,350,310	17,001,440	-20.4
6	25,620,380	20,401,160	-20.4
7	29,890,450	23,800,840	-20.4
8	34,160,520	27,200,490	-20.4
9	38,430,590	30,600,130	-20.4
10	42,700,660	33,999,760	-20.4

to cover program costs. If 25 percent of the incarcerated population were placed on a work release program, the cost to the correctional system would be cut by over 20 percent. Table 39 indicates the annual savings if this option were adopted.

Option 8: Pre-release for all parolees

This option examines the effects on the system if Ohio were to adopt a pre-release program in which all offenders served part of their sentence in prison and the last four to eight weeks in a community correctional center. Several states and the federal correctional system have implemented this type of pre-release program, contracting with private halfway houses to provide community residential services.

As can be seen from Table 40, loads on halfway houses would be enormous. Using the same percentage of assignments to the various houses, resident populations would increase by five times the present house populations, decreasing the cost to the correctional system by almost 10 percent. As can be seen in Table 41, the annual cost to the system is decreased as individuals spend the last few weeks of their sentence in a community center.

Option 9: Pre-release for 50 percent of parolees

If only 50 percent of parolees were placed in community centers the last four to eight weeks before their parole date, the results would be as illustrated in Table 42. Halfway house populations would again rise, although the numbers would not be as large as in the previous option. Again, the institutional population would drop.

Just as in the previous option, the system costs would also drop. Data in Table 43 illustrate how placing 50 percent of the inmates in community centers before parole would reduce the system cost by over 5 percent. Both Options 8 and 9 illustrate a reduced cost for the correctional system and, with adequate planning, community facilities could be developed to handle the increase in resident populations.

TABLE 40

OPTION 8: PRE-RELEASE FOR ALL PAROLEES

State	Present Load	Load after Year				
		1	2	3	5	10
1	918.0	963.7	1066.1	1131.1	1118.4	1213.4
2	8836.0	6340.6	6104.3	6062.8	6026.1	6009.9
3	386.0	280.0	267.2	265.2	263.6	262.8
4	22.2	16.1	15.3	15.2	15.1	15.1
5	226.6	280.7	291.8	291.1	290.1	389.7
6	2851.0	3671.9	3829.2	3821.1	3810.6	3806.1
7	75.0	291.4	280.1	277.4	276.5	276.1
8	19.3	127.3	119.3	117.6	116.7	116.3
9	72.9	325.8	338.9	338.3	337.0	336.4
10	10.4	66.4	63.8	62.8	62.3	62.0
11	23.9	174.2	176.5	174.5	172.9	172.2
12	94.1	326.3	321.8	321.3	322.4	323.0
13	27.0	98.4	93.2	93.3	93.7	93.9
14	33.7	102.0	100.0	100.4	101.1	101.5
15	18.3	122.0	125.5	124.5	123.5	123.1
16	15.0	91.6	84.6	83.8	83.2	82.9
17	38.4	41.1	39.1	38.8	38.6	38.5
18	222.4	290.8	306.2	305.7	304.8	304.4
19					0.0	0.0
20					263.6	262.8

TABLE 41

ACCUMULATED TEN YEAR SYSTEM COST FOR OPTION 8

Year	Present Policy	Option Policy	% Difference
1	$ 4,270,090	$ 3,905,220	-8.5%
2	8,540,130	7,770,800	-9.0
3	12,810,180	11,644,890	-9.1
4	17,080,240	15,524,500	-9.1
5	21,350,310	19,407,150	-9.1
6	25,620,380	23,291,500	-9.1
7	29,890,450	27,176,830	-9.1
8	34,160,520	31,062,700	-9.1
9	38,430,590	34,948,890	-9.1
10	42,700,660	38,835,250	-9.1

TABLE 42

OPTION 9: PRE-RELEASE FOR 50 PERCENT OF PAROLEES

State	Present Load	Load after Year				
		1	2	3	5	10
1	918.0	442.0	1000.7	1040.8	1077.2	1093.7
2	8836.0	7444.5	7236.8	7196.5	7167.0	7153.9
3	386.0	327.5	316.7	314.8	313.4	312.8
4	22.2	18.8	18.2	18.1	18.0	18.0
5	226.6	255.9	264.6	264.7	264.3	264.1
6	2851.0	3297.2	3420.6	3424.8	3421.1	3419.4
7	75.0	197.3	196.5	195.4	195.1	195.0
8	19.3	80.4	78.4	77.6	77.2	77.0
9	72.9	213.9	229.0	230.0	229.9	229.7
10	10.4	41.9	41.9	41.5	41.2	41.1
11	23.9	107.9	113.6	113.1	112.5	112.2
12	94.1	224.6	228.2	228.7	229.8	230.3
13	27.0	67.6	66.2	66.3	66.7	66.8
14	33.7	72.1	72.8	73.2	73.8	74.0
15	18.3	76.2	81.2	81.2	80.8	80.6
16	15.0	54.2	56.3	55.8	55.6	55.5
17	38.4	40.0	38.9	38.7	38.5	38.5
18	222.4	259.4	271.1	271.6	271.4	271.2
19	----				----	----
20	----				156.7	156.4

TABLE 43

ACCUMULATED TEN YEAR SYSTEM COST FOR OPTION 9

Year	Present Policy	Option Policy	% Difference
1	$ 4,270,090	$ 4,067,420	-4.7%
2	8,540,130	8,100,660	-5.1
3	12,810,180	12,136,030	-5.3
4	17,080,240	16,174,130	-5.3
5	21,350,310	20,213,820	-5.3
6	25,620,380	24,254,420	-5.3
7	29,890,450	28,295,550	-5.3
8	34,160,520	32,336,980	-5.3
9	38,430,590	36,378,580	-5.3
10	42,700,660	40,420,280	-5.3

Summary

The Markov model as presented in this chapter is a useful
tool in determining the future loads and costs of the various units
of a system under several different policy prescriptions. The
utilization of the Markov process is not limited to the relatively
small number of policy changes analyzed. These options were
chosen for examination due to their direct effect on the Ohio
halfway houses.

As indicated in Table 24, the present average monthly loads
will vary if the 1973 operations were continued. Trends indicate
that both the Federal and Ohio prison populations are rising,
leaving fewer offenders under traditional parole supervision. The
population of halfway houses will also rise for most houses, as
the current policy appears to be one emphasizing increased supervision of offenders.

When examining the various options that could occur on the
Ohio correctional scene, the results are quite informative and
suggestive. If the Ohio shock parole program would allow for
release of 50 inmates per month, the institution populations would
be reduced and the total system cost reduced by about 2 percent.
Analysis has also examined loads for regular supervision and halfway houses if shock parolees were assigned to houses as regular
parolees or if all were placed only under regular supervision.

The effect of increasing the furlough program to 30 or 50
offenders per month, and of ending the program, were also examined.
An increase in the utilization of the furlough program would lower
the institutional population, increase the number of halfway house
placements, and reduce the system cost. Ending the furlough program would, however, raise institutional populations, severly
lower the halfway house populations, and raise the cost to the
correctional system. If parole and furlough were simultaneously
increased (Option 7), the effect would would be a marked reduction
in the institutional populations and system cost.

The effect of starting a work release program in which inmates
were required to pay the variable costs of their institutional
stay has also been examined. Although there would be no resulting

change on loads, involvement of 25 percent of the institutional population in such a program would reduce system costs by over 20 percent, even after including a program administrative cost.

The final two options examined involved the use of a pre-release program in which inmates served the last four to eight weeks of their sentences in a community facility. Such a program is utilized by the Federal Bureau of Prisons with several Ohio offenders. The effect of having all, or one half of all, parolees on pre-release status would reduce the system cost by over 9 percent and 5 percent respectively. Such a program would put significant loads on halfway houses or other community facilities, although not unmanageable loads if proper planning were allowed.

Examination by the Markov model indicates that expansion of community correctional programs could be accomplished by increased utilization of halfway houses, with a resulting reduced cost to the total correctional system. It is apparent that changes in correctional policy can have a significant effect on halfway house planning.

FOOTNOTES - CHAPTER VI

1. M.A. Bell, et al., <u>Bail System Development Study</u> (Columbus: The Ohio State University Research Foundation, 1974), p. 163.

2. Data were drawn for only a one-year period (1973), and this presents a limit to the overall analysis. If possible, in future analyses, data should be collected over a longer period of time.

CHAPTER VII

SUMMARY

The preceding six chapters have illustrated the historical development of community-based corrections, the inadequate utilization of planning techniques in this development across the nation, methodological considerations for increasing the utilization of program evaluation as a feedback mechanism for planning, and analyses of halfway house data as examples of possible methodological techniques.

A brief synopsis of this monograph could perhaps be stated as: "Community-based corrections (although based on theoretically sound philosophies) has developed in an unplanned and unsystematic manner. Program evaluations have been conducted haphazardly, without supplying data beneficial to policy making. Without systematic planning based on research and evaluation, community programs are not likely to contribute significantly to the correctional process. If programs are not found to be effective, the philosophical underplanning of community programs will be criticized and programs perhaps abandoned. It is therefore important to design evaluations utilizing methods and measures amenable and transferrable to policy making." Chapters III through VI illustrate possible methods and measures for evaluation of community correctional programs.

This summary chapter presents important concerns for future developments regarding the work presented in this dissertation. From analysis of data presented in earlier chapters, conclusions will be drawn and the implications relevant for administrators and evaluators will be presented. For continued development of methodological and planning concerns, suggestions for future work are addressed. The author's review of this work could allow social scientists attempting to expand and improve the work presented herein to identify quickly the weaknesses of the study and resolve questionable criteria. Finally, implications for curriculum development in criminal justice administration are presented.

Conclusions and Implications

The analysis of halfway house data has led to several conclusions, some of which can be statistically substantiated and some of which are only theoretically defensible.[1] Without reiterating in detail the methodological procedures for drawing them, the conclusions developed from the preceding analysis are as follows:

1. The evaluative and management operations of a halfway house can be simplified by the development of measurable and realistic goals, and by outlining the perceived interaction in goals in an objective hierarchy. Chapter III points out several advantages in such a hierarchy, therefore lending evidence of its utility.

2. Halfway houses are effective treatment modalities in assisting an ex-offender in his reintegration to the community. From the analysis of outcome data in Chapter IV, ex-offenders who have experienced halfway house services scored significantly $(p < .01)$ higher on a measure of relative adjustment than a comparison group not experiencing halfway house services.

3. Results from evaluations utilizing quasi-experimental designs and dichotomous measures of outcome based on offense disposition, while not correcting for differences in experimental and comparison groups, are misleading if not invalid. Data from Chapter IV point out the fact that a significantly greater $(p < .001)$ number of the halfway house group subjects were imprisoned than in the comparison group; however, a significantly lower $(p < .003)$ number of the former had committed a new offense. These data indicate the fallibility of basing program decisions on conclusions drawn from uncontrolled evaluations using recidivism as the outcome measure.

4. There are differences in the benefit received by residents of halfway houses. The analysis of benefit (as defined and examined in Chapter V) received by house clients indicates that certain categories of residents receive a significant benefit from the halfway house experience, while data are inconclusive regarding the benefit received by others.

5. Changes in correctional policy within Ohio could have an effect on the projected loads of clients referred

to halfway houses. While simulating implementation of various policy options and utilizing a Markov model to project loads of several states within the correctional process, it is noted that halfway house loads fluctuate depending on the simulated policy.

The above conclusions point out implications important both to the administrator and evaluator in their future plans for community correctional programs. Both the administrator and evaluator, realizing the importance of developing an objectives hierarchy, should work together to formulate designs for setting and outlining interrelationships among objectives. Administrators should strive to develop program activity objectives from primary objectives before implementation of program operations. By outlining all levels of objectives to be accomplished in a program, the administrator can simplify several management and operational tasks.

The conclusion that halfway houses are an effective treatment modality for the reintegration of ex-offenders has significant implications to correctional planners and administrators. In terms of outcome indicators and financial costs, consideration should be given to the development of transitional programs for all offenders following release from correctional institutions. The use of community residential programs as an alternative to incarceration could also be expanded, with services provided to selected offenders who would normally be incarcerated. In general, a comprehensive correctional plan which maximizes the use of community residential centers should be developed.

Evaluators of criminal justice and correctional programs should also be aware of the third conclusion, regarding the fallibility of uncontrolled designs and dichotomous measures of outcome which are based on offense disposition. The problems illustrated could in part be the reason for the lack of conclusive evidence regarding the effectiveness of correctional programs. In the future, evaluators should develop more realistic outcome measures to test the effectiveness of a program in accomplishing its objectives. Moreover, outcome measures need to be sufficiently sensitive to detect gradual changes in attitude and/or behavior.

The fourth conclusion leads one to believe that halfway

houses should perhaps become more specialized in their selection and treatment of clients. Halfway house administrators should analyze the characteristics of their clients and deliberately design a program to accomodate client needs. However, specialization of services would require close cooperation with suppliers of clients (local courts, the Ohio Department of Rehabilitation and Correction, and the United States Bureau of Prisons), and would necessitate planning by suppliers in the treatment of all offender categories.

The fifth conclusion presented above points out obvious changes in halfway house loads when various possible policy implementations are simulated. The implications are significant to halfway houses; therefore, these kinds of data should be considered in any decision regarding policy which affects house operations. Policy makers should at least consider the effect of policy on houses, if not invite house personnel to participate in the policy planning process. It is also essential to consider the effectiveness of halfway houses in the reintegration of ex-offenders as an integral element in the development of correctional policy.

Future Evaluation and Research

No single study can satisfy or resolve all the questions regarding a particular topic area. Significant evaluative questions require a large-scale effort in which several authors contribute to the solution of the problem, each successive investigator building on the previous analysis. Perhaps the most significant contribution a single study can make is to identify relevant questions to narrow the scope or broaden the perspectives of future analyses.

The preceding chapters represent an attempt to present the need for evaluative research in criminal justice and correctional planning, while identifying problems which frequently occur and limit the usefulness of evaluation in the planning process. In addition, preliminary approaches for resolving these problems and making evaluation a more beneficial tool for planning and policy making have also been suggested.

The following comments reflect recommendations for future work and development of evaluative mechanisms. Utilizing the analysis and resultant conclusions of this study as a base, perceived issues and needed additions to knowledge are identified and possible types of analysis briefly critiqued.

Initially, it appears important to examine the assumption that correctional planners and policy makers are not optimally utilizing research and evaluation in their decision processes. Appropriate questions are: "To what extent are research and evaluation considered in the policy process," and "What do the users of studies suggest as improvements in evaluative designs to increase the utilization of such studies?" Simple surveys could be generated and distributed to test what has herein been assumed.

A major component of this analysis is the argument that recidivism (a dichotomous and dispositional outcome measure) is not totally appropriate as an operational definition of correctional program effectiveness. This conclusion should encourage evaluators to search for more appropriate measures of correctional outcome. The development of outcome measures is such a significant problem that additional study is mandated. While there have been efforts to prescribe continuous behavioral measures of outcome in the past few years,[2] efforts have not yet resulted in totally acceptable instrumentation. As recidivism continues to be denounced, more social scientists and methodologists undoubtedly will develop alternative measures to replace the traditional reliance on recidivism.

Another significant topic for future study resulting from this analysis are the assumptions linking objectives, as presented in the hierarchy of Chapter III. This objectives hierarchy was developed more on intuition than on research and evaluation. For systematic program planning, assumptions linking goals and activities need to be tested and, if proven valid, applied to operationalizing program activities.

Although conclusions drawn from Chapter IV substantiate the effectiveness of Ohio halfway houses in reintegrating offenders, the limits of the analysis and conclusions must be acknowledged and respected. Additional evaluations should be completed to identify further the optimal role of halfway houses in the correctional process. Further analysis of various house operations should also be completed to determine those operations most effective in fulfilling the perceived needs of residents.

A correlary need for further investigation is a continuation of the analysis of Chapter V. This preliminary effort to identify categories of residents who receive the most benefit from halfway house services should be expanded in future research. It would be useful to conduct a controlled experiment in which several categories of residents are exposed to similar treatments, and the effect of each treatment for different residents monitored. If data linking effective program activities with client categories were available, halfway houses could specialize in the type of resident selected, and design their reintegrative program around the specific needs of the resident.

The use of mathematical models (such as the Markov model in Chapter VI) should be expanded in the consideration of policy implementation. Often a policy decision will be made which may be theoretically sound; however, there may not be a sufficient population to receive services or the target population might greatly outnumber the allocated resources. Mathematical projections can be useful in the allocation of appropriate levels of resources to service clients. In the future, one could hope for a technological transfer of mathematics and systems analysis into the social welfare field.

<u>To the Future</u>

The trend toward community-based corrections has recently received severe setbacks. Certain state correctional systems and the United States Bureau of Prisons have all but ceased the emphasis or "rehabilitative" or "reintegrative" philosophies and programs. Arguing that these efforts have been no more effective than traditional imprisonment (and do not provide as much societal safety), administrators have telegraphed a return to a punishment and deterrence philosophy for treating offenders and reducing crime. This is a significant setback for advocates of reform in correctional policy who would expand the use of community corrections.

It is therefore timely to analyze--rationally and systematically--correctional policy alternatives to insure the adoption of the most effective modalities. Research and evaluation could play an important role in the future of correctional policy. Administrators now face a dilemma, torn by claims of those who advocate an increase in the use of community programs and those who favor an increase in institutionalization. History may reveal that there was never such a need for research and evaluation to provide valid information from which to formulate conclusions regarding the correction of offenders, and both administrators and evaluators should cooperate in implementing research and evaluative efforts.

FOOTNOTES - CHAPTER VII

1. There are also several assumptions which have been made and
   which undergird this dissertation. Assumptions have been
   listed in Chapter I and detailed in following chapters,
   therefore they will not be repeated.

2. David O. Moberg and Richard C. Ericson, "A New Recidivism
   Outcome Index," Federal Probation 36 (June 1972): 50-57;
   Alabama Experimental Manpower Laboratory for Corrections,
   Pacesetter 3 (March-April 1972): 1-3.

COMPARISON OF EXPERIMENTAL AND COMPARISON
GROUPS ON VARYING PARAMETERS

Parameter	Group		Level of Significance
	Experimental (N=236)	Comparison (N=404)	
Demographic Data:			
Sex (in percentages)			.08
Female	7.6	4.2	
Male	92.4	95.8	
Mean Age (in years)	31.7	30.2	.08
Race (in percentages)			.05
White	59.0	50.5	
Nonwhite	41.0	49.5	
Marital Status (in percentages)			.07
Single	71.1	76.5	
Married	28.9	23.5	
Mean Intelligence Quotient[a]	96.8	99.3	.07
Mean Educational Attainment (by grade)	9.3	9.4	.56
Criminal Record:			
Juvenile Delinquency (in percentages)			.01
Juvenile Record	46.0	27.0	
No Juvenile Record	54.0	73.0	
Age of First Offense (in years)	19.1	22.0	.01
Mean Number of Total Offenses	6.7	3.0	.01
Mean Number of Adult Offenses	4.5	2.6	.01

Parameter	Group Experimental (N=236)	Group Comparison (N=404)	Level of Significance
Mean Number of Felony Offenses	2.59	1.98	.01
Recidivistic Offenders[b] (in percentages)	92.8	70.3	.01
Type of Offense (in percentages)			
Personal	11.9	12.8	.71
Property	79.2	82.7	.28
Victimless	8.9	4.5	.02
Mean Number of Times Incarcerated	3.04	2.39	.01
Mean Percentage of Life Incarcerated	20.1	20.5	.74
Employment History:			
Mean Percentage of Life Employed	17.1	35.4	.01
Problem Areas:			
Alcohol Abuse (in percentages)			.73
Problem	33.2	32.2	
No Problem	66.8	67.8	
Drug Abuse (in percentages)			.01
Problem	21.3	11.6	
No Problem	78.7	88.4	

[a] Score by Ohio Penal Classification Test.

[b] Those with more than one prior offense.

APPENDIX B

SCORING STANDARDS FOR ACCEPTABLE BEHAVIOR SCALE

1. When considering whether employed, in school, or in training program for 50 percent of the year; the point can be awarded if any combination of the three totals 50 percent or more.

2. The point is awarded for continuous employment, school enrollment, or training even if the individual moves from one to another without delay. Also, if the individual moves "upward" in his employment (moving to a job of higher status or higher pay), he is still awarded the point. Vertical movements do not eliminate the award of this point.

3. If an individual moves from a training program or educational program to a job worthy of his training, he is given a point for vertical mobility.

4. The individual is not self-supporting if he lives with his relatives or friends and does not work. Welfare recipients cannot be self-supporting. However, if the individual is involved in a training or educational program and receives payment, he is self-supporting.

5. If an individual moves his residence at the request of a supervisory officer, or moves to a higher status neighborhood (as designated by the supervising officer), he receives a point for stability in residence.

6. Technical violations of parole or probation are considered critical incidents. Illegal activities are not critical incidents.

7. An individual can obtain financial stability and not be self-supporting. Even if on welfare or being supported by others, if he lives within his means, he is awarded the point for financial stability.

8. Self-improvement programs are defined as any effort by the individual to resolve a personal problem or improve his ability to function in society.

9. Technical violations of parole or probation are not counted as illegal activities. There is no double jeopardy for this item and item 6.

10. Satisfactory movement through parole or probation is a measure of the supervisory agent's perception of the individual's progress. It is judged by a continued reduction in level of supervision, completion of probation before the original sentenced time, or completion of Ohio parole within 14 months of release from the institution.

SELECTED BIBLIOGRAPHY

Alabama Experimental Manpower Laboratory for Corrections. Pace-setter 3 (March-April 1972): 1-3.

Bell, M.A.; Bishop, A.B.; Joscelyn, J.D.; and Marsh, J.J. Bail System Development Study. Columbus: The Ohio State University Research Foundation, 1974.

Campbell, Donald T. "Reform as Experiments," American Psychologist 24 (1969): 409-429.

Campbell, Donald T., and Stanley, Julian C. Experimental and Quasi-Experimental Designs for Research. Chicago: Rand McNally and Company, 1972.

Center for Studies of Crime and Delinquency. Graduated Release. Washington, D.C.: National Institute of Mental Health, 1971.

Conrad, John P. "Reintegration: Practice in Search of Theory." In Reintegration of the Offender Into the Community. Washington D.C.: National Institute of Law Enforcement and Criminal Justice, 1973.

Criminal Justice Digest 2 (December 1974): 1-3.

Eckenrode, Robert T. "Weighting Multiple Criteria," Management Science 12 (November 1965): 180-192.

George, J. Ann, and Milstead, R.J. "A Systems Approach to Planning, Service Delivery, and Evaluation of Alcoholism Programs." Paper presented at National Conference of Alcohol and Drug Problems Association, Minnesota, 1973.

Glaser, Daniel. The Effectiveness of a Prison and Parole System. Indianapolis: Bobbs-Merrill, 1964.

_____. Routinizing Evaluation: Getting Feedback on Effectiveness of Crime and Delinquency Programs, Washington, D.C.: Department of Health, Education, and Welfare, 1973.

Gottfredson, Don M. "The Practical Application of Research," Canadian Journal of Corrections 5 (October 1963): 212-228.

Gottfredson, Don M., and Ballard, Kelly B. "Testing Prison and Parole Decisions," 1966.

Gottfredson, Don M., and Ballard, Kelly B. The Validity of Two Parole Prediction Scales: An 8-Year Follow-up Study. Vacaville: California Department of Corrections, 1965.

Gottfredson, Don M.; Ballard, Kelly B.; and Bonds, J.A. Base Expectancy: California Institution for Women. Sacramento: Institute for the Study of Crime and Delinquency, and California Department of Corrections, 1962.

Guba, Egon G., and Stufflebeam, Daniel L. "Evaluation: The Process of Stimulating, Aiding, and Abetting Insightful Action." Address delivered at 2nd National Symposium for Professors of Educational Research, Columbus, Ohio, November 21, 1968.

Hayner, Norman S. "Why Do Parole Boards Lag in the Use of Prediction Scores?" Pacific Sociological Review 1 (Fall 1958): 73-76.

Hitt, William D. "Management by Objectives in Educational Systems." Memorandum.

Huber, George P. "Multi-Attribute Utility Models: A Review of Field and Field-Like Studies," Management Science 20 (June 1974): 1393-1402.

Logan, Charles. "Evaluative Research in Crime and Delinquency," Journal of Criminal Law, Criminology, and Police Science 63 (September 1972): 378-387.

McCartt, John M., and Mangogna, Thomas J. Guidelines and Standards for Halfway Houses and Community Treatment Centers. Washington, D.C.: U.S. Government Printing Office, 1973.

Mannheim, H., and Wilkins, Leslie T. Prediction Methods in Relation to Borstal Training. London: Her Majesty's Stationery Office, 1955.

March, James G., and Simon, Herbert A. Organizations. New York: John Wiley, 1958.

Martinson, Robert. "What Works?--Questions and Answers About Prison Reform," Public Interest, no. 35 (Spring 1974): 22-25.

Miller, Stuart J. "Post-Institutional Adjustment of 443 Consecutive TICO Releasees." Ph.D. dissertation, The Ohio State University, 1971.

Milstead, Robin J. "The Use of an Objectives Hierarchy in Planning, Operating, and Evaluating Halfway House Programs." M.S.W. paper, The Ohio State University, 1973.

Moberg, David O., and Ericson, Richard C. "A New Recidivism Outcome Index," Federal Probation 36 (June 1972): 50-57.

National Criminal Justice Information and Statistics Service. Criminal Victimization in the United States. Washington, D.C.: U.S. Department of Justice, 1974.

Ohio Adult Parole Authority. Furlough Program Guidelines. Columbus: Ohio Department of Rehabilitation and Correction, 1973.

O'Leary, Vincent, and Duffee, David. "Correctional Policy--A Classification of Goals Designed for Change," Crime and Delinquency 17 (October 1971): 373-386.

Powers, Edwin. "Halfway Houses: An Historical Perspective," American Journal of Correction 21 (July-August 1959): 20-22,35.

President's Commission on Law Enforcement and Administration of Justice. Task Force Report: Corrections. Washington, D.C.: U.S. Government Printing Office, 1967.

Reckless, Walter C. The Crime Problem. 5th ed. New York: Appleton-Century-Crofts, 1973.

Rivlin, Alice M. Systematic Thinking for Social Action. Washington, D.C.: The Brookings Institute, 1971.

Rothman, David J. The Discovery of the Asylum. Boston: Little Brown and Company, 1971.

Seiter, Richard P. A Statistical Model to Test the Effectiveness of the Ohio Halfway House Programs. Columbus: The Ohio State University Program for the Study of Crime and Delinquency, 1972.

Sellin, Thorsten, and Wolfgang, Marvin E. Measurement of Delinquency. New York: John Wiley and Sons, 1964.

Simon, Herbert A. "On the Concept of Organizational Goals," Administrative Science Quarterly 9 (June 1964): 1-22.

Solomon, R.L. "An Extension of Control Group Design, " Psychological Bulletin 46 (1949): 137-150.

Sullivan, Dennis C.; Seigel, Larry J.; and Clear, Todd. "The Halfway House, Ten Years Later: Reappraisal of Correctional Innovation," Canadian Journal of Criminology and Corrections 16 (April 1974): 188-197.

Sutherland, Edwin H., and Cressey, Arnold R. Criminology. 8th ed. Philadelphia: J.B. Lippincott Company, 1970.

Warfield, John N. An Assault on Complexity. Columbus: Battelle Memorial Institute, 1973.

Warren, Marguerite Q., et al. Community Treatment Project: An Evaluation of Community Treatment for Delinquency. Fifth progress report. Sacremento: California Youth Authority and the National Institute of Mental Health, 1966.

Weiss, Carol H. Evaluative Research: Methods of Assessing Program Effectiveness. Englewood Cliffs, N.J.: Prentice Hall, Inc., 1972.

7